MW00477698

Anxious **MOM,** Anxious **CHILD**

A Mother's Journey from Anxiety to Serenity

Adacelis Pérez

**Breathe
Publishing**

Anxious Mom, Anxious Child
August 2018
Breathe Publishing, Inc.
ISBN 978-0692160480
www.BreathePublishing.com

*To my Mom, who has taught me through
her example the meaning of unconditional love.*

CONTENTS

Introduction   1

SECTION I

*My Journey to Serenity after Divorce
and Illness*

Chapter 1.

Playing in the Sand   13

Chapter 2.

Healing My Heart   29

Chapter 3.

Connecting with My Son   65

Chapter 4.

Within My Soul   95

Chapter 5.

Breathe Away the Pain   107

SECTION II

*How I Created a Deeper Connection
with My Child*

Chapter 6.

Build a Bridge   145

Chapter 7.

Teaching through Example   163

Chapter 8.

Ahead of the Wave   185

Chapter 9.

Masters in Disguise   211

Acknowledgments   227
References   229
About the Author   231
Index   233

INTRODUCTION

The room was dark and quiet, and I was finally ready to close my eyes and declare this day over. Lying in bed, I looked at the time. It was a few minutes past 10:00 p.m. My mind was blurry and my body felt like it was crumbling beneath my head. I was beyond exhausted. Suddenly, a series of overwhelming emotions came over me like a giant wave, not the kind that is soothing and calming, but the kind that crashes into your face at once and makes you feel like you are about to drown.

I was home and could almost feel a sense of relief, but a week before I had been excited about going away for a few days. I was headed to Puerto Rico with my eight-year-old son Lucian for a short family visit. It had been over a year since I last visited with my family and a lot had happened on the island since then: an enduring financial crisis, the battle against the Zika epidemic, and two devastating hurricanes, Irma and Maria, the latter of which ravaged the island, leaving over a thousand dead and millions without power for months.

I wanted to feel useful during my stay, so I offered to take my mom to the car dealership so that she could have the birthday present that her beloved Martín wanted to give her.

"Mom, can we go get the new car on Monday?"

Mom had an eye doctor appointment in the afternoon, so we'd have to make the purchase rather quickly. Monday came and off we went. A few hours later I had accomplished my mission. The new car looked great and my mom was happy. I had saved the day. Yet three days later I was driving her new car into a wall.

A simple request by my son Lucian to use the bathroom had sent me through the roof. "Lucian is not a baby, I expect him to do better than this," I thought. The rush of blood climbed up the right side of my neck, wrapping slowly around the sides of my face; my head felt warm and heavy – I was about to explode. "Why didn't he use the restroom before we left the house?" I was thinking and overthinking. I stared at the wheel, trying to stay focused on the road. In a few minutes, I was dealing with disaster.

I didn't mean to, of course. I just missed seeing a three-foot concrete wall in a parking lot, not a big deal. My internal dialogue started: I didn't know the area well, it was a tiny parking lot and it was crowded … Why on earth was the wall there in the first place? Well, at least it was only a scratch … I made up excuses, but I knew I was wrong.

In that moment, I was embarrassed and so mad at myself, but I had to focus and keep driving. In fact, I had to keep driving for the next hour and ten minutes because we were scheduled to take a flight. Perhaps I should've handed over the wheel, but I felt I needed to correct my own wrongdoing and end the trip on a high note by driving us safely to San Juan. I had been there before, in the middle of a situation that I had to erase from my memory. I changed topics in my mind and focused on something else: the weather outside, the clear sky with playful clouds and the blue shades against the sun, the beauty of the scenery rising majestically as if settling matters plainly. I began my routine of looking at things from a perspective that made me feel better, my immediate go-to hiding place and a prerequisite to emerging sane and unscathed from a crisis. I felt guilty but also relieved that I was able to keep my cool throughout the ordeal.

The events of that day in Puerto Rico are an example of a seemingly simple situation that can throw an anxious mom like me into an overthinking mode. Regardless of where anxious thoughts like these came from, I must admit I was the one channeling them and creating a space of tension in myself. Beyond the effect those thoughts had on me, they could've created a chaotic energy around me, a burden for others and my son to carry.

The line of thinking that kept things together when adrenaline was rushing through went like this:

1. We are on time, but we are unaware of traffic conditions.
2. The sooner we get on the highway the better.
3. My child needs to go potty and I don't know where to stop for a bathroom break.
4. I need to take him to a bathroom, and it needs to be now.
5. It's fine, we'll be back on the road and on our way to the airport soon enough.

In between those orderly ideas, there were a million agonizing thoughts of fear and anxiety running through my mind. But I was resolved: "I can overcome. We will make it on time."

A couple of hours later, we boarded the flight and were on our way back home. Lucian plugged in earphones and quietly watched the television. I was relieved that we had made it to the flight on time. For Lucian, luckily, the whole "accident thing" was just a fleeting moment on a hectic day.

Back home that evening, as I dozed off, I hit the play button on my cell phone to ease my mind and help me go to sleep. I listened to a meditation video, the type that can rescue me after a difficult day. The gentle voice of the narrator and the soothing tones in the background helped me get there ... *"If these feelings are not yours, you can let them go."* As I listened and let myself become more and more relaxed, I sought answers to my questions:

"Whose feelings are these? Whose anxiety is this? Am I the one creating the overwhelming feelings of fear that seem to take over? Where do they come from, these feelings?"

I sat with the questions. I knew I was responsible for my behavior, and the absent-mindedness of that moment when I hit the wall was my own wrongdoing. I felt responsible for these feelings of loss of control, rush, tension, and uneasiness. I was not sure where these feelings came from: me, the Universe, or other souls who were traveling nearby. Somehow, thinking that they were not mine made me feel better. I continued to breathe deeply, counting to four, releasing and counting again—one, two, three ... four. Soon I was sound asleep.

I needed to challenge these feelings, regardless of whose they were or where they came from. For all I knew they were mine, and I needed to come to terms with this side of me that haunted me and exhausted my life at times. It was not my son's responsibility or my mom's responsibility or the world out there that I needed to blame. It started with me. It had to stop with me.

The next morning, I decided to let it go. I recognized the cloud of tension still floating above my head. I closed my eyes and said a prayer. I asked God for clarity, for his light to cover me, to go beneath my skin to the deepest corners where the most inner feelings of fear resided.

"Shine a light in the deepest corner of my soul and return my being to peace," I prayed. Praying is one of my favorite allies when I struggle with being overwhelmed by emotions. It is one among many other tools that has helped me tame my anxiety.

"*Ada, Ada* ..."

I talked on the phone with my mom, and we chatted about what had happened the day before. She reminded me what I already knew. I needed to take control. She delivered the message with compassion, her voice gentle but stern. The tone was familiar to me. It was the tone that tells instead of asking, that shoots straight like a dagger but enters your skin like a petal. The tone that demands action, yet respects your free will. Mom has a way of giving advice with intention, with a wealth of experience and wisdom. Her words have the ability to sound light yet heavy, exposing what was not said as much as what *was* said, by the silence in between, and making you aware of the pounding inside as your heart recognizes the truth in them.

Thankfully, those days of struggling with my anxiety are gone. These days I'm able to detect the triggers and swiftly put my plan into action to calm myself down; I'm happier and healthier. Even though I'm aware that the anxious modes could come back, they can't control me anymore.

HOW I HOPE TO CONTRIBUTE

There are a plethora of books about healing obsessive thinking and anxiety. For those who suffer from debilitating anxiety, cognitive therapy along with other forms of treatment may help overcome the specific type of anxiety that affects them. I'm not a medical expert, but I suggest that those who experience severe anxiety seek treatment to alleviate their symptoms.

For those imperfect but awesome moms who are trying their best (I'm one of them), I'd like to offer some ideas that may help ease feelings of generalized anxiety. In my case, anxiety has shown up as obsessive negative thoughts and stress. Furthermore, I'd like to offer advice that may help nourish the mother–child connection through moments of serenity and tenderness.

I wrote this book to unburden myself from some of my most intimate emotions, to heal from wounds that have caused a great deal of anxiety for me, and to share what I've learned throughout this process. Research suggests that children in the United States are increasingly affected by anxiety—because of home dynamics and because of external factors that parents have little to no control over—but we seldom hear about the possible negative effects that a mother's anxiety can have on her child.* In fact, a recent study shows that there might be multigenerational effects for women who suffer from anxiety.**

Anxiety can affect our ability to create meaningful, calming experiences that promote effective conversations at home with our children, our spouse, and others outside of our family. When we are anxious, it is hard to communicate effectively because we feel overwhelmed by emotions. The symptoms of anxiety usually stem from our fear, but they can manifest as anger toward those around us. Anxiety can dampen our ability to listen attentively and understand how our child is feeling, keeping us from being able to connect and build a strong bond with them.

When we address our anxiety, we can find out exactly what the triggers are, so that we can stop the fearful or angry feelings right at the moment when those emotions are rising within us. Through constant discipline, we can establish ways to detect those triggers of our anxiety and move past them. When we move past those emotions, we are able to have meaningful interactions with our children, and we learn about their feelings, thoughts and concerns.

As we learn to move beyond anxiety and worry, we can replace our anxious tendencies with more calming expressions. We can protect our children so they don't become the victims of tension and stress. I hope that in sharing my experience, I can respectfully add to a wider conversation about anxiety among mothers and the impact that their anxious behavior can have on their children.

The book is organized in two sections. You can choose to read the first section first or you can dive in to the second section, where you will find strategies and advice for dealing with anxiety.

SECTION I.

In the first section of the book, I share my experience growing up in a coastal town in Puerto Rico. I believe that the values I learned growing up in a close-knit family, enjoying plenty of time outdoors playing unstructured games with childhood friends, combined with a strict education, have played an important role in my healing. I recognize the relevance of the lessons learned during my childhood, especially in today's increasingly hectic world. Therefore, I reflect upon my childhood in order to share thoughts and ideas about the core values that every child should learn early on: a sense of belonging, a feeling of safety, unconditional love, respect, and compassion toward oneself and others.

SECTION II.

In the second section of the book, I share insights about how anxiety manifests in our daily routine. I offer ideas and advice for mothers who might be struggling with feelings of stress and anxiety. Through mindfulness, patterns of obsessive thinking and worry can be reversed and replaced with a calm demeanor, so more effective communication and a deeper connection can flourish between us and our children. In this section, I also look ahead to challenges that face our children in this modern era of the internet and social media. Finally, I suggest methods that moms may use to help our children navigate through this era of rapidly changing technology and learning environments.

My hope is that through my personal experiences, ideas and exercises shared in this book, you will be able to do the following:

- Recognize signs of anxiety that may be affecting your relationship with your child.
- Use the strategies shared in this book to calm your anxiety.
- Be more conscious about the tone, rhythm and space you are creating around your child.
- Have more intentional conversations with your child.
- Feel a deeper and more meaningful connection with your child.

I am aware that getting rid of anxiety completely might be next to impossible. It is normal for a person to think ahead and worry at times about the future as long as it doesn't become a burden that disrupts our peace of mind and our relationships at home and with others.

After suffering from anxiety for close to seven years, I've learned how to calm down my obsessive thinking tendencies and reduce the amount of stress in my home. Like me, other moms might be struggling with anxiety. Getting our patterns of obsessive thinking under control is possible.

When I became aware of the emotions that caused my anxiety, I embarked on a journey that led me to discover my inner fears, which led to profound insights and new ways of looking at my mental habits and emotional landscape. I was faced with many decisions, including the decision to take medication to calm my anxiety.

One benefit among many is that calming down my anxiety has improved the quality of my interactions with my son. Being aware of the triggers that cause me to feel anxious has made me calmer, and I don't react on impulse. When I am calm, I can be a better listener to my child and connect with him at a deeper level.

As a more attentive mother to my son, I am prepared for the years ahead when the noise in our environment (the increased use of technology and the pressures of young adulthood) will affect him in ways I can't imagine. The many lessons from my journey have translated into concrete ideas, motherly advice, and useful practices I'm sure will help him thrive.

I invite you to read the stories from my childhood and from a more recent past as an anxious mom who has struggled constantly with patterns of obsessive thinking and generalized anxiety. More importantly, I hope that, as you put into motion your own plan for healing from anxiety using the various techniques that I share in this book, you also can feel that you've got your anxious modes under control.

Making the decision to pay attention to the triggers that cause anxiety, and acting to prevent them from coming back, can lead us to changing habits that are not serving us. When that happens, not only can we live a more peaceful, joyful experience, but most importantly, we can shield our children from unnecessary drama and stress. We can do this!

Section I

My Journey to Serenity after Divorce and Illness

1

Playing in the Sand

Who am I in the middle
of all this thought traffic?

— Rumi

I watched as Lucian ran downstairs in the chilly winter morning and waited for our ride to the airport to arrive. He was wearing the blue jeans and long-sleeved shirt that he'd reluctantly agreed to put on earlier that morning, his attitude compliant as he moved swiftly through our home. The mood was orderly but slightly tense as I tried to get things ready before we left home for our vacation. The rhythm of a day like this brought an additional burden for Lucian: having to endure his stressed-out mom.

"It's okay, Mom. I don't want to make you nervous."

The most condescending comment that my child had ever made rang true. A few minutes later, the Uber driver pulled up in front of the garage, and soon enough we had loaded our luggage into the car and were headed to Atlanta's Hartsfield–Jackson Airport. It was a smooth drive, the roads were clear, and I could've been enjoying the music on the speakers or the sky outside my window. Instead, I was mulling over the truth of Lucian's words. He knew better than to get on his mom's nerves on certain days, like when we were preparing for a big event. He needed to comply or he would meet the might of his "Mean Mom."

Those were the times when the "Mean Mom" would show up, when the coldness in my voice would threaten and the fuming look in my eyes would meet Lucian's fearful face. Who is this woman? I'd look in the mirror after one of those episodes and not recognize myself. He is eight now, but there were times when I didn't have enough patience to deal with this little boy who had such a strong personality. When did children become so hard-headed? I'd wonder. I was struggling. I would've preferred a child that I could direct in every sense of the word. As a baby, he was a joy. As a toddler, however, he was defiant, yet gentle and sweet. He was sensitive and dramatic at times, and his tantrums—nothing I could've been prepared for. I needed to get things under control, otherwise I would fail miserably. I was determined to remain the ruler in my kingdom of fear.

I know very well what a kingdom of fear looks like because I'm a product of one. My mom, a strict Catholic, had a bachelor's degree in pharmacy and a master's in discipline. AKA someone to be afraid of. Her techniques throughout the years worked because, as they'd say, my two brothers and I didn't turn out that bad. We went to college, graduated with degrees and went on to have decent and productive lives. Admittedly, not only have we come out "okay," but the three of us are deeply connected and devoted to our mother.

It would be natural that as my mom's only daughter I would try to emulate the qualities that I saw in her. However different I thought I was from my mom, and even when I swore that I'd never be like her, time would prove me wrong.

For starters, I think I always thought my mom was much more beautiful than I am. Not that she ever made me feel less pretty, and I don't think that I would've recognized it when I was growing up, but secretly I thought my mom was gorgeous. A gentle face with almond-shaped brown eyes that were never unkind. To this day, she has aged gracefully, but I hang on to my memories of her when she was my age: her soft, shoulder-length, thick dark brown hair, her delicate nose with the right proportions, her face like a heart with cheekbones perfectly placed. Mom had the right measurements in every regard. Her style was unique at times, but always conservative, and she enjoyed dressing up in elegant gowns when it was time to go out to fancy events with my dad. When someone who knew my mom said to me, "Oh goodness, you look so much like your mom!" I didn't believe them. Not because I didn't want to be compared to my mom, but because I felt we were so different. "I think I look more like my dad," I replied. From a distance, my mom and I didn't look much different; we had similar frames, petite and slender; we both had brown eyes, brown hair, and light skin. If you looked closely, however, you'd notice that my face was broader and my cheekbones more pronounced than hers. Though my eyes were almond-shaped, like hers, I had wide eyelids, almost Asian-looking. I never thought of myself as ugly, but if given an option, I think I would've chosen my mom's features over mine.

My mom was beautiful not only on the outside, but on the inside as well. She was dignified and kind—kind to the point of naiveté. That type of kind. While she was a strict mother, something that made me feel at odds with her sometimes, I see now how much of her there is in me. And the mom in me often goes down memory lane seeking to borrow her tips and advice, like checking in the imaginary Encyclopedia Britannica for clues about parenting. How would my mom handle this? What would my mom do about that? I consciously never wanted to be like my mom, but as I've grown older and wiser I see how I *should* have been more like her. We are worlds apart in terms of personality, which might be the reason I didn't feel that I had a close relationship with her during my childhood.

As I grew older, I identified more with her older sister, Estella. She was tall and graceful and had porcelain skin that shone from a distance. With features similar to my mom's, Aunt Estella had a much livelier personality. A total extrovert, sometimes to a fault, Aunt Estella would say what was on her mind—always. Her voice was strong, her sense of humor witty, her mind sharp. She was the one who rebelled against her dominant father at a time when women were expected to stay put and follow the lead of their elders. At the age of twenty, after studying business in San Juan, she decided to move away from her parents' home in Puerto Rico and try her luck in the United States. While my mom "followed the rules," went to college and earned an enviable degree in pharmacy, married and had children, Aunt Estella was independent-minded. She worked full-time throughout her adult life. She ventured into a new career when many women her age were getting ready to retire, and she offered to take care of her sister, my Aunt Jenny, who, after suffering an accident when she was a toddler, lost some of her mental faculties. To this day, I call Aunt Estella for her advice on life, her outlook on things, and her wise words have helped me endure my angst. The best cook in her family, she remains the strongest personality among the three sisters. Maybe I got her genes. Maybe my son Lucian did, too.

GROWING UP AN ISLANDER

I could never have predicted that I'd suffer from stress or anxiety. Growing up in the coastal town of Arecibo, I lived in a laid-back environment, with two pharmacists as parents.

My family on my dad's side owned a pharmacy, which had been in his family since the 1950s. With a lot of effort, my grandparents had bought the business from the previous owner. It must have been a given that my father would continue his dad's legacy as head of the "botica," as they use to call the drugstore. Deep inside, however, being a pharmacist was never a dream of my dad's. In spite of this, he did the best he could to make it a successful business and a meaningful career, and to provide for his wife and three children.

In the house where I grew up, the medicine cabinet is still in the very same spot: on the left side as you enter the kitchen, all the way in the corner next to the wall that leads to the hallway. The refreshed medication collection sits quietly on the top shelves. The newer laminate-covered cabinets have replaced the old wooden ones that kept medications safe from our intrusive hands. In those days, medications didn't come with all the labels and safety features of today; just orange plastic bottles with flat white plastic tops, easy to open. Yet however easy they were to reach, we knew we'd better check with Mom or Dad before attempting to have some.

From syrups to tablets and capsules of all sizes, shapes and colors, you could find a remedy for any ailment. If you had a headache, there was ibuprofen. If you had a sore throat, Chloraseptic would save the day. You'd spray your mouth every four to six hours and feel the relief within a day. Any time one of her three kids was sick, Mom would come to the cabinet and pull out what seemed to us like a magic formula. Conversations about diseases and about the treatments to cure them were frequent in our home. My mom and dad shared stories about the latest product development news and trends in pharmacy, which they had read in the most recent edition of their pharmacy publications.

Some of the fondest of memories I have of my dad are from the late 1970s. I must have been five or six years old, but the images of the routine went on for years: I would hear the keys jingle in the back door as he arrived home from work in the evenings, and I'd run to the door by the kitchen to meet him. In a race to get to the door, our dog Muffin, a poodle mix with ivory fur, would often beat me. Every day as Dad opened the door, he'd quickly pull out a piece of candy from his briefcase for me and my brothers. He knew exactly what I liked. It was usually my favorite, peanut M&Ms. The yellow bag was a treasure in my hands.

While I can't trace the face of my dad in those days, I can still remember the smell of his uniform, which reminded me of air conditioning, plastic, and cotton balls. I can picture the rows of small white boxes sitting nicely along the rows of shelves in his "recetario" where all the medicines were stored in the back of the drugstore. His uniform was always the same, a white button-down shirt with pockets, a couple of pens peeking out of the corner, dark pants and boat shoes, though not the fine leather ones. He would sit at his desk at home and often continue working for hours after dinner—his days were long. His little girl wanted to hug him as he finally lay down to watch TV every night.

On Sundays, Dad would sit on the sofa reading the paper. Daddy's only girl would often come and sit next to him. He'd hand me the cartoon section, which I thoroughly enjoyed. *Peanuts* and *Mafalda* were some of my favorites. My parents knew everything there was to know about prescription drugs, and they would often talk to us in detail about whatever drug was prescribed when one of us got sick. Antibiotics, for example, were a good thing, but when taken too often they could "kill the good bacteria in you." This I would learn the hard way many years later, when I suffered from candidiasis, an overgrowth of yeast in the digestive tract.

I remember thinking at the time that it was a good thing to know so much about how to treat an illness. When my friends were feeling unwell, I'd ask what their symptoms were and suggest a treatment for them. Nowadays I can make the connection between my familiarity with drugs and my early exposure to topics such as mentally debilitating issues and their treatment.

"Las medicinas no son golosinas" (Medicines are not candy), read the poster that hung on the wall by the counter at

my family's drugstore, a warning for those who might contemplate abusing medication. The round glass container held multicolored candies: blue, red, yellow. New Drugstore, or Farmacia Nueva, was the name of our family business when I was a child.

I had, in my view, such a fun childhood in my hometown of Arecibo. Raised by a loving and devoted mom and a hardworking dad, I attended Colegio San Felipe, a Catholic school run by Hermanas de la Divina Providencia, or Sisters of the Divine Providence. There I met the kindest yet toughest nuns, who imparted discipline "with a smile," so to speak. The most prestigious private school in my hometown was, for the most part, like any private school: structured enough, yet never too closed up to the world outside.

I remember them clearly. They would say the morning prayers over the microphone, and we would all stand up, looking at the wooden box hanging on the wall, and reply, "Good morning, Sister." Most of the teachers were kind and generous, although they had to keep as many as 30 students in one classroom quiet, without an assistant teacher, so their generosity and patience had its limits.

My mom was extremely patient as well, but she had a temper. With an older brother, a younger brother, and me in the middle, we completed the trifecta, and I know my mom didn't have it easy with the three of us to look after. She was a strong woman, devoted to her family and to God, and she knew how to make us follow her lead. We had chores at home, and we were part of youth groups at church. A frequent volunteer at the local parish, she had us attend mass every Sunday.

"At least your mom didn't have to work full-time like I did, Ada," my godmother Sophia would say with a quirk in her smile. She was the wittiest of our neighbors, my mom's best friend and my godmother through Confirmation. She and my mom were pregnant at the same time and went to pregnancy classes together. Sophia lived four houses down the street from us.

Years later as we grew older and were able to better understand the nuances of adult conversations, we'd remember how she would sometimes tell my mom that she had it easier. Even back in the 1970s when women were joining the workforce as professionals in high numbers, there will still plenty of those women who, if given the chance, would've preferred to stay at home raising their children. My godmother Sophia worked all her life as a teacher, and I remember wondering how she was able to manage work and her home life. She and her husband both worked for over 30 years as teachers. They are now happy retirees living in North Carolina, where they chose to emigrate so they could be closer to their daughter Camila and their grandchildren. Camila was my very best friend growing up, an almost-sister to me.

My mom was always there for us. Like her mom before her, she was a devoted wife and a stay-at-home mother for the most part. Although she worked part-time at the drugstore, she was dedicated to her children. She'd wake up bright and early, her voice filling the air with spiritual songs. I don't remember a sound of an alarm clock, but I do remember having mixed emotions over the morning ritual on weekdays when there was school.

As sweet as her singing was, I always wanted to stay in bed. When her singing wouldn't persuade us, she would try something less gentle, like pouring a little bit of water over our heads. The sight of her hands with the cup filled with water as she stepped into my room would be enough to make me jump out of bed in a flash. Looking back, I can't judge her. She'd wake up early to make us a really nice breakfast—oatmeal and fruit, or hard-boiled eggs with toast and milk—and she didn't like it when it got cold.

Dad would take us to school, then she'd pick us up at 2:30 and we'd go home for a snack. After a snack and homework, we had the rest of the afternoon to play outside with our neighbors. We were three active kids: Louis (the eldest), David and me. We loved playing outside with our friends, some of whom we've stayed in touch with to this day.

I wasn't an athlete or a musician, but I considered myself a poet. I enjoyed reading and writing the most, and when I was in fourth grade, I won a national poetry competition.

My favorite line of the poem went like this: "*The smile is a gift, it's more than a gesture. It's a token of love, that culminates in a kiss.*" (*La sonrisa es un don, es algo más que un gesto. Es una muestra de amor, que culmina con un beso*).

How did the personality of a poet, an analyzer and a dreamer reconcile with the outspoken, mischievous part of me? I have no idea. I could never have imagined that the lively girl and adventurous young woman I was would turn into the anxiety-ridden woman I became. I remember having a lot of stories conjured up in my head, and I'd write poems in the solitude of my room, late at night or early in the mornings or on weekends. I'd hide the notebooks filled with pages of poems and essays and stories that I'd tell myself. I also kept journals. I remember one in particular that had a tiny lock attached to the cover. I wanted to keep everyone away from my stories, which at the time might have been mostly about silly arguments with my girlfriends at school or about the boys I had a crush on. I had to keep everyone away from my thoughts, especially my two brothers, both of whom I had to fight off sometimes with fists and hair-pulling fights.

For the most part, however, we got along and we played with each other and with our friends from the neighborhood. Going outside every afternoon after doing homework was the best part of our day. We'd run from one front yard to the next, making up stories and games, hiding behind Cruz de Marta bushes while sipping the juice that the flower kept inside. The tiny cross-shaped flower had a small stem that we'd pull out and lick—a tiny drop of delicious nectar within our reach all year long.

At the time, life in my hometown of Arecibo was pretty uneventful. The tropical weather of the Caribbean allowed for year-round adventures that could take us to a hike in the island's rainforest, *El Yunque,* and a dip at the nearby beach, both on the same day. My mom would get all the kids in the dark-cherry-colored Chevrolet wagon with a spacious wide trunk that allowed for two or three of us to sit back there. Our trips to the beach have a special place in the collection of memories from my childhood. My favorite bathing suit displayed the power of my heroine: Wonder Woman. I'd climb up the rocks in the shallow waters and jump down with my best friend, Camila, who was the same age. We must have been six years old at the time. The Polaroid picture that remains in my photo album from childhood tells the story of those days and takes me back to that very spot: the light sand sitting peacefully, four-foot-deep clear water with barely any waves. We'd sit under a palm tree where the moms waited with enough food to feed an army. Godmother Sophia would make our favorite dish of hers, her own version of fried rice. The taste of soy sauce mixed in with the sprouts, pieces of egg, and chicken floating throughout made for a feast.

Our trips to the beach never came before our duty with church. Mom made sure that we made it to mass, even when we were vacationing on the opposite side of the island, in the Eastern city of Fajardo. Our destination: Isleta Marina (Marine Island). It sat a mile from the coastal town and could be reached by visitors and residents via ferry.

Every year, I'd look forward to our vacation on Isleta Marina, usually during spring break. I thought it was the coolest thing—being tucked away on a remote island was the greatest of adventures for a curious little girl like me. The ferry ride was my favorite part. I would always sit by the window and look down on the deep blue waters, impenetrable and scary. My mind would imagine sharks and all kinds of fish looming under the surface.

Once in Isleta Marina, my two brothers and I would run down a long path that led to the beach, palm trees standing on both sides as if guarding pedestrians from the heat of the sun. Louis is three years older than me. David, my younger brother, was more of an introvert and shy at the time. As we grew older, things slowly changed, and the two brothers would eventually have opposite personalities from what I remembered them to be. Louis would become mostly an introvert as a teenager, although still vivacious. He had a good heart and always carried the burden of being the "oldest one." Louis was energetic and active, while David, who played with me more often because we were only one year apart, would become more outgoing and more of an extrovert as a young adult. We were very close and we all had similar features, except for David, who had the most beautiful blue eyes. They could turn gray or green depending on the shirt he was wearing. Cat eyes. I'd wonder why I didn't get eyes like his. The three of us were dynamite, full of energy and never too tired to go play. We loved the outdoors, especially the beach.

The view of the ocean from the tall tower of condos in Isleta Marina displayed a magnificent spread of shades of blue. The beach was perfect for young children, because the water sat so low you could walk yards into the ocean and still see your toes as you ventured away from the beachside. When we didn't want to walk, we'd wear our snorkeling gear and head down the small pathways of rocks and plants like seagrass and algae. It must have taken years for the path to become so perfect; it was quite the underwater adventure for us. We'd follow the tiny fish swimming quickly around us, trying to catch them with our fishnets.

My dad would sit in a folding chair close to the water, holding the newspaper in his hands, his fair legs deep in the water. A few hours later, he'd gather us around and start a fire in one of the iron BBQ stations, where visitors would start their grilling sessions early in the afternoon. Dad's favorite was chicken and steak skewers, Puerto Rican style. The smell of burnt coal was quickly forgotten after the first bite of the freshly grilled meat.

Rain seldom ruined our vacation stays in Isleta Marina. The sky was clear and bright during Easter week, which offers the best of temperatures in the Caribbean and virtually no sign of mosquitoes. The palm trees provided the perfect spot to rest from the bright light that caused such glare you'd have to be covered in sun block to keep from burning. My mom was an expert at keeping us safe that way. The smell of coconut lotion to this day brings me back to that beautiful place. These memories of our family trips to the beach are the fondest of them all. I wonder if my brothers feel the same way.

My mom thought I was the rebellious one of her three children. I was outspoken and sometimes just plain loud. I hated her disciplinarian ways and I let her know how I felt. I wonder if my mom ever pictured me as a mother. I'm sure it would have been hard to reconcile that image with the mischievous Ada, smart in academics and skillful in the arts, unruly and boisterous at times, yet always willing to participate in activities at church, chorus and youth groups.

I was in sixth grade when the matter of manners became very important at school. I was reminded of them by one of my brightest teachers. Her name was Mrs. King.

"Where is your handkerchief?" she would ask. Her dark curly hair framed a tanned and wide face. A few gray hairs were already showing, telling the story of an experienced teacher who knew how to get unruly children back in line. She was adamant about keeping us from "spreading the germs" in the classroom. I compare it to the relatively relaxed environment of my son's school today, and I think he has it easy. I like to tell stories of my childhood to Lucian, sometimes just to get a kick out of his reaction.

"Son," I tell Lucian, "you have no idea how awesome your life is."

"I guess I'm lucky that I didn't go to your school," Lucian replies, smiling.

I'm only half joking, of course, because I had plenty of fun times at school. A wide rubber tree sat as the centerpiece of the schoolyard. Its wide trunk had bulky veins that came down to the ground where it would meet the layer of concrete that surrounded the tree. We'd play under its copious shade during recess and lunchtime. Rubber trees date back to the pre-Columbian era, and some species date back hundreds of years in their native South America, but they are also found in the Caribbean Antilles. The image of that tree and the childhood circle games and laughter shared under its welcoming shade always brings a smile to my face.

"Lady Helena was in the ball, let her dance, let her dance" (*La señorita Helena estando en el baile, que lo baile, que lo baile*), one of the songs would go. There was always lots of singing during girls' hand-clapping games. A sign of good times, a sign of a worry-free existence.

2

Healing My Heart

Where can I go from your spirit? Or where can I flee from your presence?
If I ascend to heaven you are there; if I make my bed in Sheol, you are
there. If I take the wings of the morning and settle at the farthest limits
of the sea, even there your hand shall lead me, and your right hand shall
hold me fast.

— Psalm 139:7-10

"Maybe the reason why you and Marcus got married was to bring your son Lucian into this world," said Elliot.

His voice was soft and the look in his eyes comforting. I was sitting on a wooden bench by a fountain in the garden of the retreat center. Tears were rolling down my cheeks as I listened to the words of the man of faith sitting beside me. I was in my late thirties, I was a single mom with a baby, and I had just gotten divorced. The message that he was trying to convey was not an easy one to receive. I wasn't expecting spiritual advice from a stranger, but his words, I could tell, carried a deeper meaning. As if they were opening the door to a new understanding of my reality, a more spiritual perspective on events. His words touched a very sensitive part of me.

I had more than one revelation on that weekend, and to this day I feel that the breakthroughs for me, from a spiritual point of view, were life-changing. By the second day of the silent retreat I knew why I had to be there in the first place.

It was October, which in Georgia is a gorgeous time of year, with a sea of yellow, red and brown colors and leaves falling from the trees like potpourri.

In normal circumstances, I'd be unable to keep my active mouth shut for more than ten minutes. But by the grace of God, I joined the group of close to 50 women and kept quiet throughout almost the whole time. I say "almost" because there were a few moments when I broke away to chat with my new friend, Elisa. I met her on the first day during introductions. She was a delightful Dominican lady, soft-spoken with gentle eyes and a heart of gold. As the weekend wrapped up, I noticed that something in me had changed. I felt that I had met with the deepest of fears and had uncovered a big piece of my inner truth. "Going there," spiritually speaking, was not easy.

Ignatius House is a retreat center that sits at the top of a hill about twenty minutes from my home. Its lovely grounds abound with trails that lead you to the Chattahoochee River. There is a small waterfall that's like a treasure you find after you've been digging for hours. I fell in love with this retreat center and to this day I visit it often.

There is a special place in my heart for spiritual matters, and exploring my spirituality has made me a wiser mother. The process of healing continued after my retreat. I was going deeper, learning more about myself every step of the way.

It has taken years of self-exploration, of reading countless pages of advice from gurus, watching thousands of hours of online self-help videos, going to therapy and undergoing treatment, and saying daily prayers, often with tear-filled eyes.

FROM SMALL TOWN TO BIG CITY

My curiosity about the world around me and my love for reading started at an early age and continued through high school. I was always a good student with mostly A's, and learning new things, especially anything to do with art or writing, was always fun.

When I was a senior in high school, far from feeling anxious about graduating, I was excited, elated and so looking forward to it. Unlike many other kids my age during that time, I felt I would be able to finally break free from home and leave the life in my hometown of Arecibo, which at that point I felt had become too small for an adventure-seeker like me. I was ready to take off and dreamed of having a full life in college with thousands of students like me, roaming the campus of a grand university. I couldn't wait to experience the big city of Río Piedras.

I can't recall a time during those years when I felt that anxiety was affecting me, because during those years I didn't have much to worry about in life. The only sign might have been that I never stopped shaking one of my legs, which I was told recently is a sign of anxiety. It might be a simplistic view in hindsight, but I think I was the typical student who made a lot of friends and enjoyed chatting in between classes. I may have been a bit distracted, but nothing to be worried about. I was lively and eager to learn about new things, and curious about cultures different than mine.

What I thought would wait for me was a world wide enough to fit my ideas for a life of travel, adventure, and learning. I had visions of places that I never had known. I still have clear memories of my father sitting down in the living room of our home reading with interest the latest edition of his favorite monthly magazine, *National Geographic*. It must have been from my father that I got interested in places afar, cultures that seemed taken from a history book, images so vivid that made me want to dive in for a splash with the whales, or dance with the natives in faraway lands such as Africa or Indonesia.

The pages of the *National Geographic* were clear in my memory, the yellowed frame of each issue encapsulating a new discovery: the remains of the Titanic, the Afghan girl with the piercing green eyes, the African tigers, lions or elephants that were being threatened by extinction, courageous climbers that sought the tops of the highest mountains under extreme weather conditions. I was fascinated by the images and the seemingly hard-wired content of these stories. I wanted to be inside of them all.

Looking back at the time when I used to read my dad's magazines takes me to bittersweet memories of the time when he passed away. I was in my early twenties when the car that he was in hit a wall on the side of the road in the early hours of a Thanksgiving Day. It was 1995 and he was only 51. The whole event of his passing and the way it happened was life-changing for me. What pains you are able to carry, you will never know until you've experienced losses and grief that are so unexpected, unapologetic, coming through like the blow of a hurricane, smashing everything you had built. The castle inside my imagination, the one that had stories of princes and fairies and happy endings, was smashed by the terrible, sudden passing of the first man that I ever fell in love with.

I often wonder how my dad would've been as a grandfather. I'm sorry that his journey ended so soon. He was an imperfect man in some regards, not always the best husband to my mom. He had a strong temper, but he also had a fun-loving side that we often got to see. He worked really hard at the drugstore and would often have us come to help. While he didn't actually say the words "I love you" often, if ever (back then it wasn't the way men were raised to be), he set a good example at home and showed us what being a man of service in the community looked like by volunteering his time to nonprofit organizations. His duty as a father was fulfilled, at least from my point of view. I wonder what he would've thought of his curious little grandchild. I hope he is watching from somewhere, laughing I'm sure, at the funny things that Lucian can come up with.

I've carried on my father's desire to explore, and my decision to move to Atlanta in 1998 would lead me to experience a great many adventures that I only dreamed of when I graduated from college. I had decided, against the advice of some, to move to Atlanta from Puerto Rico. I had a very stable job at the time, at the oldest bank on the island, Banco Popular de Puerto Rico. The bank offered a stable salary and great benefits.

It was also close to my mom's, so I could head home for lunch and come right back to work. After a little over two years on the job, however, I started to feel like retail banking was not the right fit for me.

With my background in mass communications, I dreamt of being surrounded by media gurus, and I especially wanted to travel, see new scenery and learn about different cultures. I found all that and more in Atlanta. Throughout the years that I worked at Turner Broadcasting System, I was able to expand my horizons in every sense of the word. Not only was Atlanta a growing city at the time, it was only two years after the 1996 Olympics, and the vibe was one of expansion with an influx of new industries. I was lucky to land that job at Turner, and while there were years of climbing up the corporate ladder (the new generation could learn a thing or two about patience), I felt that I was learning a whole lot. I felt even luckier to be able to travel throughout Latin America with journalists. I was their publicist, handling affairs from behind the scenes, looking after the network's image at all times. I was a representative of a brand, and I can honestly say that I believed in everything it stood for. I was able to visit Argentina, Brazil, Colombia, Chile, Costa Rica, Jamaica, Mexico, and Venezuela, to name a few. I attended events up close and from behind the scenes, like conglomerates of presidents who joined in on conferences like APEC (Asia-Pacific Economic Cooperation) in Chile and the wedding of the Prince of Spain (now King Felipe and Queen Letizia). I got to meet famous people like the internationally renowned author Gabriel García Márquez and celebrities like Jane Fonda, Ricky Martin and Julio Iglesias, plus Atlanta's own Ted Turner.

One time, on my way back from an international trip as I arrived at Atlanta's Hartsfield–Jackson Airport, I met Elizabeth Gilbert, who at the time had just released her popular memoir, *Eat, Pray, Love*. She was sitting on a bench, and I walked up to her after recognizing her from the multiple interviews and videos that I had seen on TV and on the internet.

I thought it was interesting to help support the work of numerous talented journalists, including international reporters who risk their lives often and expose themselves to human horror away from their families and their children—Christiane Amanpour, Arwa Damon and Nic Robertson, to name a few. I have special fond memories of my travels with some of them: Patricia Janiot, a leading news anchor who was committed to transparent journalism, always fearless in her interviews with politicians; Glenda Umaña Hidalgo, endearing in her appearances on TV and in person, she brought important messages to journalism students at talks in her native Costa Rica; Ralitsa Vassileva, a Bulgarian journalist whom I became fond of after our trip together to Mexico City where she led an audience at an international leadership conference; and Jonathan Mann, a Canadian who would ride his bike to work even on the hottest of days; these are some of the CNN anchors that I had the pleasure of collaborating with as their publicist during special reports and events on-the-ground throughout Latin America. Some of them just had a special way that made them shine through the TV screen, a special kindness in their voice, a heart of gold that could be seen outside of the roles on TV. José Levy, who at the time reported from the Middle East, always brought wooden rosaries from Jerusalem when he visited Atlanta. Others, like Daniel Viotto, Harris Whitbeck and Rafael Romo, were calm and collected in the middle of a crisis. All of them were serious about their roles and devoted to delivering the news in an unbiased way. My years at Turner led to many adventures, and I felt proud of working alongside a group of talented professionals from diverse backgrounds and from various nationalities, all of whom believed deeply in the importance of serious and truthful journalism.

Twelve years after I moved to Atlanta and about eleven years after joining Turner, I gave birth to my adorable son, Lucian.

Early on, we could tell Lucian would be a strong-willed fella. A few days after he was born, I struggled with breastfeeding an always-hungry baby; the routine became demanding but I was elated to have the experience of breastfeeding my newborn.

As the baby got bigger, he was energetic and was slowly turning into an adventurous toddler. He loved going to the playground at the nearest park, climbing up and going down the slides, easily coming up with games and joining other kids on the playground. I'd encourage him to make friends. He was rambunctious, sometimes shy, always sensitive and kind. Lucian had a lot of energy and his naps were short. His tiny legs moved quickly around the house, ready to play ball of any kind, at any time, on any given day. He met all his milestones and was keeping us busy.

My little boy has shown me the brightest hours of my life. I remember my morning ritual with baby Lucian. When he was a newborn, I used to sit in a bright orange rocking armchair in his bedroom, a gift from his Grandma Charlotte. You could be swallowed by the soft fleece-like fabric for hours. My favorite time of the day to be with him in that very spot was in the mornings, when the bright sun entered through the window where the armchair was. I would look outside while holding my beautiful child and feel as if I was in a perfect place, like a dream. The world seemed to stop; the quiet mornings would have me staring at him, feeding him and showering him with soft kisses. Looking down, I would cherish the view of his soft tiny hands, his round face and brown eyes framed by long eyelashes that to this day can melt my heart in an instant. It was perfection.

What wasn't so perfect was the amount of stress that I began to feel soon after Lucian's father and I separated. It was late 2010 and it was the beginning of a very difficult time.

That stubborn fog in my life took seven years to clear. The desolate cliff saw me standing alone, arms out, facing the wind like Kate Winslet in the movie *Titanic*, except that I wasn't Kate Winslet and I wasn't on the bow of the Titanic. I'd be standing on top of the cliff, wondering how things would have been if my decisions had been different. How would our lives be if I was still married to my son's dad? I can now look back and, even though there are moments when I wonder, I've found a place of contentment, right here in my very present set of circumstances. The spiritual work that I've done throughout the past has paid off.

The minutes, hours, days of mindfulness, of practicing yoga, of exercising regularly, of listening to the advice of friends and family. The endless conversations that helped me reflect on my mistakes, and the passage of time, have helped in this process. I can see now how my efforts to stay present for my son have taken our mother–son relationship to a new level of connection. His needs have been met and I feel as if we have landed on the other side. I've averted many crises that could've erupted if I hadn't gotten my anxiety under control. I've won the battle. Or should I say I've won *one* battle against anxiety? Buried deep in my soul was the fear that I wasn't as good a mom as I could have been. That fear was joined by a sense of guilt over not having made it through a marriage so that he could've had a more traditional experience in his life. Yet those fears and its companions don't have as much weight anymore. They are triggers to my anxiety, but now I am able to recognize them.

Before they take hold of me, I'm able to tackle each fear individually. I breathe in and I breathe out. I face the fear head-on and almost talk to it. I replace the fear with the truth. I like to focus on the wonderful moments with my child, like, for example, Lucian's smile as he gets out of the car to go to school, his stories about a new game or a song, when he shares ideas to help resolve a problem at home, and even the cute phone conversations with his best friend at night. I also think of his proud moments—when he has scored a goal, when he got a perfect score on a spelling test, and most importantly, his joy when he knows that we are getting together, all of us: mom and dad and grandparents and close friends, as a modern family. I remind myself of everything that is beautiful and true in my life and I move past the fear. Soon enough, I forget that fear was there in the first place.

GETTING STILL

Attending the silent spiritual retreat was the beginning of an intense journey to the depths of my soul. It was fall of 2014, and I had lost my job. After working continuously for over 15 years, I now had time to take a break, a much-needed break that would allow me to work on myself and be with myself. I was exploring new territory.

What to do with all this time? The spiritual journey led me to go deep, really deep inside myself, to face and heal the wounds of my divorce. To face the reality of my decisions and the pain of the breaking up of a family—my family. I had to heal the wounds of being hurt deeply as a wife and as a woman. I had to learn to forgive my ex-husband, for I'm sure that I had hurt him as well. I also had to forgive myself for not being who I thought I had to be; and I had to make peace with the person that I am.

It is precisely because I'm divorced and have lived alone with my son for many years that I've found time and space to examine where I've been, the decisions and the choices that I've made which have brought me to the very place that I'm in right now.

Shortly after my divorce seven years ago, I read a book called *Spiritual Divorce* by Debbie Ford. The book encouraged me to look at the positive side of the ordeal, the idea being that it isn't such a terrible thing to endure, and that after a marriage there is hope for starting all over again. I remember that, for the first time, I was looking at divorce in a lighter way, validating the truest of feelings which had been neglected for so long even by me, and finding new perspectives that were liberating. In many ways, I was giving myself permission to start over. The difference is that starting over when you have a toddler is not as easy, and it shouldn't be. Life has a completely different focus, and your priorities as a mom can turn the priorities of the past upside down.

I had to make adjustments, and I had to make sure that I was providing for my son in a lot of ways. I wondered if, with only one parent, my son would be lacking in things that he would never be able to have. Would he grow up missing an important element that would affect him forever? I tried to make sense of my new reality and arm myself with messages of strength from authors, women like me who had endured the process of divorce and had survived it. The messages were healing, yet there were days during those four or five years when my son was a toddler and a preschooler when I felt that the pressure was brutal.

The daily routine felt at times like enslavement. It was me, day and night, dropping off my son and picking him up from school four days a week, making sure his clothes were ready and the house was clean, cooking, and giving him a bath. It was mostly all me. Fortunately, Lucian's father has done his best to be present in his son's life. Lucian and his dad are very close, they have a special bond and I couldn't be more grateful. While we've had our differences through the years, it has been a relatively cordial and friendly relationship.

Divorce and co-parenting, however, brought unimaginable exhaustion, pain, sleepless nights and long days that never seemed to end. Even many months after my divorce, I felt that I couldn't concentrate on my job. I tried very hard to stay focused, but I couldn't.

My mind would wander to places that it hadn't gone before, from fantasies of having the perfect family unit with the house and the white picket fence, to facing the cruel reality of a new financial situation that required me to work harder and see my son less than I wanted to. It wasn't fun to discover that my new reality as a single mom had some pretty rough edges, like rocks in the river. My new life was uneven, gray, soft and flat, heavy and sturdy; it would sit at the edge of the waters to watch as dreams would go by, touching it, leaving it behind. I was in for a grand spectacle of fear.

One Sunday afternoon, I was talking on the phone with Martín. I was sharing my thoughts about a conversation with a friend from the day before, listening intently in anticipation of the wisdom that Martín's words would impart.

Martín was born in 1920 in Arecibo, and he was married for 60 years before his wife, Flora, passed away from cancer in the early 1990s. He was an ophthalmologist, an agronomist, and a long-time Rotary member whose leadership and good deeds had earned him the respect of both his peers and the younger generation. Aside from having the longest life of anyone I know, Martín has the most awards that I have ever seen in one room. There are certificates of collaboration, mounted wooden plaques, letters of appreciation for extensive work that he has done over the years with organizations such as Rotary Club International and the Asociación Médica de Puerto Rico (National Medical Association of Puerto Rico), among many others. Dr. Iguina Mora, as he is usually called, embodies a man of honor. A veteran of World War II, he can tell you stories of the years before my mom was born in rural Puerto Rico. He is my mom's best friend and her companion. When Martín talks, everyone in my family listens. Martín is in his 90s, yet his mind is sharp with an unbelievable intellectual capacity that we greatly admire.

On that afternoon, I explained to Martín that a friend had mentioned how he admired his sister because she had "chosen wisely" when she got married. Which had me wondering like a maniac why on earth I had chosen to marry Marcus and why he had chosen to marry me. I said to Martín, "I don't understand why it bothers me so much, that conversation?"

His response was simple: there was nothing about that conversation that should bother me, for in fact, I had freely chosen whom to marry. The simplicity of his response, concise yet profound, carried the knowledge of those who have lived a long time. Even though his words came from a place of compassion, they didn't sound tender to me. I was taken aback, and at first I didn't appreciate Martín's viewpoint. However, as I thought about his response more closely, I realized he was right. I wasn't a victim. I had made a decision and I had to deal with the consequences of my actions. I told myself, "Deal with it, Ada." His words would have to console my lunatic comings and goings, the constant revisiting of the reasons why I chose to marry and why I chose to divorce. These obsessive thoughts often follow some after they divorce.

EXPLANATIONS FOR LUCIAN

I got divorced when my son was just over a year old, and since then I've been in countless conversations with friends where I've had to justify the reasons I'm divorced. A few years ago, it was especially painful to have to answer the questions posed by Lucian, who by age six was an expert at coming up with the most interesting questions about the world around him:

"What happens when birds die, Mom? Where is your dad? I mean, is he in heaven?"

Lucian's questions about death always took me to that place in my mind where I seldom wanted to go. He started asking questions about life and death around the time a neighbor found a dead bird in the front yard. Also around that time, Lucian started noticing the family pictures in the house. I would often point to people in the pictures and tell him who they were. Family pictures from years ago would offer me the opportunity to tell him stories of my childhood. My father, who of course was in the pictures, became a topic of our conversation one time. It wasn't easy for me to talk about his death, and I remember that I explained to Lucian how some people have one idea of what happens after we die while others have completely different ideas.

"I like to think that we go to a happy place when we die," I would say. But I don't know for sure. "Nobody knows."

Sometimes I'd ask Lucian what he thought happened to us when we die. I wanted to be careful not to imprint my own thoughts about life and death. I remember clearly that when we had this conversation about life and death for the first time, we were in the kitchen. I asked, "What do you think happens when we die?" Lucian responded, "I think we come back alive?"

I didn't want to read too much into his response, but I wondered, where did he get the idea that we come back alive? Was it a fluke, something he just came up with? I remember thinking that I wanted to be careful with my response. A definite response that painted a sad picture of events after we die could have a lasting effect on my son's life. What if he becomes afraid of death? I certainly didn't want him to be afraid of dying, so I decided to leave it up to him to decide what happens. My stance on the subject, every time it came up, was the same. He seemed satisfied with my response and with the images he came up with.

Lucian was in first grade when he started to ask the dreaded "divorce questions." Soon after, the questions become more specific: "Why did you and Dad get divorced?" I was prepared to answer these questions. I had read about it extensively, and decided that I wanted to call my son's dad for a family meeting to talk to Lucian and address this very question. The meeting never happened, but I looked for moments when I could calmly discuss the topic of divorce with Lucian.

"Dad is your husband, right, Mom?"

"No, Lucian. Dad used to be my husband, but now we are friends."

A few weeks later, the questions came up again. The next inquiry told of a longing for something that Lucian wanted but couldn't have.

"I wish you and Dad would live in the same house."

"I know, Lucian."

I'd answer in the warmest tone possible. I would acknowledge Lucian's feelings and then I was quiet for a moment. My heart would feel so heavy every time I had to address the topic of divorce and living separately.

Responding to the divorce question is hard because you feel that you want to be truthful but you don't want to hurt their feelings. As a single mom you are reminded of your situation as a "one-man show," at times feeling inadequate when among families of two parents. Not all the time, and this doesn't last forever, but there is a period in your life when you are adjusting to your new reality.

Fortunately for me, my son was young enough that he barely remembered when his dad and I split. The pain of getting a divorce, however, extends to many areas, and for an anxious mom like me, being divorced has added to the collection of negative thoughts that accumulate and begin to slowly fester in my mind.

Like millions of women who have endured this painful situation, I didn't want a divorce. What divorce brings is the opportunity for two adults to willingly go their separate ways with the hope that they can find peace; the bond that once united them is dissolved, and they will try to find happiness again, on their own or next to someone else. For parents, the decision to get a divorce represents a huge burden: the back-and-forth of taking the children from one home to another, the mental exhaustion of negotiating terms, the bitter arguments that must happen at a time when the children are not around, the endless coordinating of schedules—all the while making sure that the physical and emotional needs of the children are met. It isn't too different than two-parent homes, when you think about it. The challenge is in handling it on your own. Regardless of the reasons why the divorce came to be, sometimes it is the child who will bear the burden of the parents' decisions. The challenges that come with managing a home and a child by myself have brought many stressors to this divorcee.

"Don't do it," I'd say, finding myself giving the anti-divorce advice to a friend. She had been arguing bitterly with her alcoholic husband and finally reached a breaking point. The smart lawyer that can win every argument had become exhausted with the ongoing battle. I told her one time, "Don't tire of loving, my friend."

Soon after, I learned that she stayed and decided to work things out with this man whom she still deeply adored, even after all the troubles of the past. They have an adorable child together and have overcome many challenges.

"I brought this on myself," I told myself sometimes. And the overthinking onslaught would come again. I analyzed and overanalyzed my own broken marriage. Comparing one's situation with someone else's has proven to be a profoundly useless and severely detrimental exercise, so I decided to leave it alone.

Alone indeed, I alone had to figure out how best to manage my life for the sake of my young child. I know that parents who are married also have numerous struggles, and that children who seem to be thriving might be experiencing profound sadness as they witness the bitter fighting between their parents. I sit at numerous dinners with my married friends who complain endlessly about the state of their union, with financial disputes, cheating scandals, family dramas that permeate their whole tribe … I listen. I imagine what it must be like to be the children in those homes during those bitter exchanges between adults—from clashes over the best way to discipline their children, to disagreements over the number of activities their children participate in, to different views of religion and spiritual values, to attitudes toward spending, and many others. Even though children may be resilient by nature, sometimes as parents we fail to shield them from disagreements, from the wrong comments we make in phone conversations that they can hear, or from the things that we know we shouldn't do but still do in front of them, all of which can shape their minds and change who they are.

We can seed fantastic stories of wonder and dreams in their minds, with hopes for an unimaginably amazing future, with continents of experiences that are available outside the window, if only they follow our advice—if they make enough effort at school, follow the family schedule, play music and sports and chess, take tae kwon do and learn to speak a foreign language or two. If only they can get the perfect friends, from the perfect family, and avail themselves of the most appropriate and pristine experiences in our society, and if they can be wary of the evil that surrounds us.

I contemplated the options for my son and I tried to stay on track. I tried not to indulge in assumptions of the future, but to stay in the approachable and fragile present moment.

It was no easy task, especially for a mom like me, who takes a tour around the planet with overthinking patterns that can exhaust even a pavilion full of cheering fans at a World Cup. I had a major task at hand just trying to be there, in the city of Atlanta, in my home, worrying about doing laundry and breakfast, lunch and dinner. Looking beyond my immediate needs was a daunting task; in-depth analysis of the state of affairs in my life, with the probability of a disastrous future, was not something that I wanted to engage in.

It must have been year number two after my divorce, and Lucian's morning tantrums could still drive me to crazy town. His crying in the morning while I tried to get him dressed could be heard from across the hallway. One morning as I tried to dial in to a conference call, I was feeling the pressure.

"I can't concentrate!" It was only me in the house with my young son, so I would talk to myself. On the other end of the line were members of three marketing teams who sat on the other side of the world, literally. Europe, Middle East, and Asia, respectively. Trying to concentrate on a conference call while changing the diaper of your crying toddler is not a rewarding experience. Lucian was refusing to wear shoes or shorts, or a shirt, for that matter. Stressful. Add to that the lack of a full night's sleep four days in a row and you have a life spent of much-needed energy. You are about to break. "Marcus, can you please keep this child, please?" I'd call for my ex-husband in silence. My married friends would tell me that I was a "lucky one." I couldn't understand what was so great about my circumstances.

"At least you get a break from your child," Annette would say jokingly as we discussed the logistics of co-parenting. Smart and wise beyond her young years, Annette is witty and light-hearted, a petite figure with enchanting blue eyes and long dark hair that frames her beautiful face. She's a professional and a mother of two. I enjoy listening to her practical advice about career, life and parenting.

Friends like Annette meant the world to me during the first few years after my divorce. With my family miles away, their advice and friendship meant everything. Just having another adult in the room made such a big difference, and usually those conversations would stay with me for days. I'd look back and find hidden messages, honest advice that felt like a thoughtful present. The kind that you can't get at the store. Some days, however, I would retreat to my home and just sit quietly with myself. On those days, what I really wanted was a break from my feelings of being lonely and trapped.

TAKING MEDICATION

"No way!" I told myself a million times over. I could never have imagined that I would be one to take antidepressants. I had heard that "crazy pills" should only be used as an extreme solution to mental issues, for those who were in "really bad shape." Not me. The idea became less threatening and more familiar after I moved to Atlanta in the late '90s. Love them if you will, hate them if you must; I have a love–hate relationship with my meds. I stopped taking them recently and I feel victorious, but my experience of taking medication to treat depression or anxiety is something I want to share because there is a lot of stigma around the topic.

"¿Como estás? (How are you?)," my favorite physician of all time would greet me with a warm smile. Her name was Dr. Nevarez, and she was from Spain. Her pronounced Spanish accent, with her "s" sounding more like a "z," would welcome me as she reached out to shake my hand. She immediately made me feel at ease. A bright woman with a great sense of humor, she wasn't your typical physician. She was a mature lady, sophisticated, in fashionable attire. She never wore a uniform with a stethoscope around her neck. Her approach was gentle, her advice practical and on point. I later learned that she was a mother and a grandmother of twins. Her comforting words reminded me that my angels had not forgotten me, that they'd sent in some help. It had been a few months since my divorce was finalized, and I was considering the dire circumstances of my state of mind. Dr. Nevarez recommended that I take anti-depressants, and as unwilling as I was, I realized that I might want to take the advice of this qualified someone whom I happened to trust.

"Antidepressants?" I had noticed how the lack of sleep was affecting me, and she recommended that I give them a try. I struggled with the decision because I felt that I might become addicted to medication.

Deciding if I should start taking antidepressants wasn't easy. With all the information that I had been exposed to since childhood, including stories of terrible side effects, I had a lot to consider. In the end, I went along with Dr. Nevarez's recommendation. I began treatment and it went well; I was able to sleep and had more energy. There were days, however, when I didn't like my treatment so much. Having a glass of wine made me feel a little funny, and I didn't want to feel like I depended on something to feel better. I remembered times when close friends had shared their experiences taking antidepressants. I had judged them severely because I felt they could be treating only symptoms and not the core of an issue. I feared that they'd be signing up for addiction. Yet, I was feeling strong, like I was over the hump of my divorce.

After a few weeks, I had to acknowledge the treatment was helping. According to Dr. Nevarez, aside from the death of a close relative—a child or mother or father—going through a divorce is the number one cause of stress that can negatively affect a person.

I had been taking antidepressants for about eight months when I started to feel funny about them. I was having the sensation of feeling removed from things that were happening around me, as if there was a distance between me and the experience: a delayed response to my active listening, a certain slowness in reaching states of gladness. My perception of things was different at that time. So I made a decision: although medication was helping me deal with the sleepless nights, I was feeling spaced out, so I wanted to stop taking it.

It might be confusing to some, but if you have suffered from anxiety and have struggled with the decision of taking antianxiety medication to ease the symptoms, you might be able to relate to the process that I found myself in. Yes, I'm glad that I could afford to have access to them when I needed them the most. Yes, I'm grateful that antidepressants can help on many occasions to keep my anxiety under control, but knowing that they exist makes me feel like there is an easier way of dealing with this maddening condition of existence without making a bigger effort.

Another reason I felt conflicted was because of the stigma that is sometimes attached to the use of antianxiety medication. I wasn't comfortable sharing my struggle with depression and anxiety with friends and family. For some, taking antianxiety medication as prescribed by a doctor is a no-brainer. As over-prescribed as they might seem in our modern society, antianxiety medications help, especially when other areas in our lives such as sleep or concentration are affected. Those who have a less positive view of the effects that chemicals can have on our bodies are concerned that one might become dependent on medication. Others, especially in certain circles that are skeptical of modern medicine, feel that taking antianxiety medication implies "mental illness" (or other less charitable terms). The truth is that the disorder of anxiety can be treated successfully with antianxiety medication if the person decides that this is the route they want to take. My main issue was getting an answer to this question: how long will I have to take medication?

I loved how medication could help, but I hated that it helped me that easily. The Christian in me was coming out, demanding I be punished for taking the "easy road" as opposed to the more torturous one.

I would find myself wondering, "Am I supposed to suffer a bit to get out of this mess? Or is the suffering that I've endured enough?" If there is a magic pill to treat my anxiety, why bother going through each and every one of the thousands of minutes that it takes me to breathe deeply, meditate, exercise, and make countless visits to physicians and therapists. Why bother?

The problem is that they work. I realize that I'm exactly on the fence here. While I can relate to those who swear by the benefits of taking medication to treat their symptoms of depression or anxiety, I'm aware of the side effects. I'm glad to know that so many mental health issues can be effectively treated with medication, and I've benefited from its use, but I still feel uneasy about it. The orange plastic bottle sits on my kitchen cabinet staring at me every morning. I make the decision to leave them alone or to invite them in.

Can I go without them? If so, for how long? Will taking them prove that I'm not equipped to handle my anxiety? Will continuing with this treatment mean that I am giving up on other treatments for anxiety? The truth is, taking the medication for a while felt like the raising of the white flag for me. It felt like I was conceding defeat. "But I'm not a wimp and I didn't get to this point in my life by giving up this easily," I'd debate with myself. Since when did I give so much power to a bunch of compounded chemicals in the shape of a pill?

"In other parts of the world where there is less access to antianxiety medication, people seem to survive just fine," I tell myself, as I go back and forth in my mind. The truth is that these tools can help and *do* help, and when people are in crisis they should be able to get treatment if this is what the doctor has recommended.

Maybe it is up to us, the patients, to determine how much "power," if you will, we will give to this type of treatment. For me, and I can only speak from my experience, there is a balance that I've tried to reach. I don't like absolutes and I'm not one to describe situations in terms of black and white, because life is not as simple as that. Life is full of grays.

ON A SUNNY EASTER SUNDAY

"Auntie Ada, come watch me fly my kite."

It was year number seven after my divorce. Amanda was ten and she stood in the doorway of the kitchen in her home, her print dress delightfully displaying an array of bright colors under the early afternoon sun. It was an Easter Sunday in full bloom, its color showing its glee in every garden across my friend's lovely traditional ivory brick home. As we stepped outside to the front of the house I could feel the warmth of springtime on my skin.

Amanda's kite was almost as tall as she was, I noticed as she stood by the kitchen door that led to the front of the house. She waved the large white and gray dragon, with a golden yellow heart at the center of the kite. I don't recall ever having such a fancy kite when I was growing up. I was fascinated by the dragon's wide wings with a tail that dragged along the floor, a few feet long.

I was stepping outside my good friend Elizabeth's beautiful home in the suburbs of Atlanta. The big lawn was before me now, the sun was joyful, a few trees were showing their new sets of leaves after a long, if not that cold, winter, and I was feeling like I wanted to run after Amanda's kite. I was ready to join the fun when I realized I was wearing the wrong shoes. As I took a step further, I felt the heel of my designer pump sink deeply into the grass. But the skeptical looks of the adults around didn't stop me from following the lead of this 10-year-old. Her little brother quickly followed her on the grassy front yard; his colorful kite was just as large. Blocks of orange, red, black, and yellow floating in the air, the long tail flipping as it began its parade above us like a rainbow dancing and jumping from one cloud to another.

Down below on the plane of the earth where this mortal stood, my heels sank deeper in the dirt as I pondered whether I should miss the moment with the little ones to save my shoes. My mind was calculating the risks of damaging my shoes while analyzing the amount of dirt that was sticking to the long three-inch heels. "Are there rocks that could scratch the leather heel? What about the front of the shoe? Was the tip getting muddy or was it okay? Should I step a little to the side where there is more grass and less dirt, or should I walk toward the concrete so that I can walk safely along the edge, outside but not in it?" The kids were waiting; they called to me again so that I could join them, and I was about to make a swift decision.

My mind was pondering what to do while my tongue was busy responding to my mother's insidious questions on the phone. My Easter greetings would soon become an argument when my mom's comments went from conversational to judgmental. I quickly changed the subject and reminded my mom that our philosophies about certain things are different and that by now she should know better than to reprimand me … I'm old enough to treat my elders with respect even when I feel like screaming at them. How many women in their forties fear the disapproval or disappointment of their mother? Am I the only one who is very aware of the everlasting expectations of our mothers even as they grow older? Am I the only one who listens to their sometimes loving yet critical advice? Ah, yes, I'm sure I'm one of them. I adore my mom so much, and the fact that she lives thousands of miles away doesn't make her less able to intrude and opine even when her advice was not requested.

I wondered if my inclination to obsess over thoughts stemmed from genetics. I wondered if this was one more thing that I owed to the one person that I've loved the most in my life.

I made the decision as I paced in the front yard that I wanted to enjoy the kites for a little, while the slow stream of adults headed inside to savor the delicious Easter brunch that my friends had prepared. A few minutes later, I joined the adults. The kiddos didn't fly the kites as long as I would've wanted them to, but I was glad to have stepped outside.

Back inside, I navigated the dining area and the kitchen. I sipped my mimosa and grabbed a bite to eat, I had fun conversations and smiled, and I was genuinely happy to be there among those faces that I knew so well. I felt consoled in a way … it hadn't been the best day so far, I realized. In fact, it hadn't been the best of weekends for me. The stream of stories that I was telling my friends was coming down from a mind that had been full of worrisome situations in recent days, such as when I had learned that a neighbor was suffering from breast cancer, and a high school friend feared that she had a brain tumor. Along with this were concerns about impending new contract work which might require that I travel more often, and the state of my personal projects that required a major effort, like the writing of my book; all of these had gotten me in a "funk," and I let them loose with some restraint. I could sense my blood traveling through my veins faster, boiling up in my system as my efforts to contain the spill failed. I told my friends about the conversation with my mom. I was sitting down now, across the table from friends; we joked and I laughed about the little things that can get to us. We moved from one topic to another, and before I knew it, I was sharing the story that had been bothering me since the morning: I had forgotten to bring the right shoes to go to church.

I had also forgotten to take my antidepressant. Were these crazy thoughts the consequences of my own wrongdoing?

"No one will be paying attention to your shoes, Ada."

My boyfriend Gerard, a gentleman with a bright smile and a kind soul, had tried to make me feel better. I had been complaining a couple of hours before on our way to church. Surely my concern over shoes seemed liked the most ridiculous of issues to worry about. Maybe he was on to something, but I couldn't hear him.

The turmoil inside was slowly building. It was less because of the shoes and more about something else. The series of thoughts looming on the outskirts of my soul were slowly making headway. I sat in the back of the church, trying to concentrate on the task at hand. The choir was singing beautiful songs of Christ's victory over death, as I mentally crawled to the tomb asking God for a break.

Sitting with my friends, I looked around the manicured table with tulips and bunnies and shades of pink and violet and yellow and white. I tasted the labor of love by the hosts, enjoying deviled eggs sprinkled with green onions, potato salad and the smell of squash casserole nicely topped with crumbled bread crumbs, the sounds of chatter, of a family gathering peppered with laughter, mimosas in fluted glasses that brightened up the space, seeing the friendliest of faces whichever way you turned.

I spent the rest of the afternoon in a relatively calm state of mind, but the unwanted visitor seemed adamant in his intent to push me harder, to be sure to get a hold on me. A few hours later as we dined with the family, I had my official breakdown. I cried and I let loose. I put words to describe what had been bothering me. Surprisingly, I was not the only one in the room feeling completely overwhelmed on that weekend. Once again, around a beautiful table and surrounded by kindred hearts, I regained my strength and continued on, moving beyond the obsessive thoughts that lingered. There are moments when everything stops in your mind, and you hear the voices of those sitting next to you from afar. You are in a cloud, it seems, yet you are sitting right there. You come back to your mind and rekindle your connection to your own body, and you succeed. You smile because smiling always helps. Laughter, that's the cure. You are back, and you are in control again.

Spring is my favorite of the seasons, allergies aside. The birds sing louder, perhaps because I missed them during the winter. The season of green is here and I can see the trees slowly dancing. The carpenter bees playfully fly above the rose bushes that are coming back for a new season. I appreciate the changing of season because it's a reminder that everything in life is temporary. The most dreadful of feelings are also temporary. I take a deep breath and imagine the bright sphere of light coming down from the top of my head, pushing through from the center all the way down to my neck, splitting and spreading on each side to cover my arms. The light continues to push my darkest feelings out of my body, all the way down; my chest feels lighter as the light continues down my lower back, my thighs, and my knees, until it makes it to my feet. I imagine myself pushing these thoughts out of my body through the soles of my feet. I let them go.

LETTING GO OF NEGATIVE THOUGHTS

While my anxiety issues were not debilitating enough to keep me from going to work, the stress of balancing my professional life and my home life became such a burden that I often had trouble falling asleep. I couldn't concentrate on certain tasks at home, and I had a lot of trouble being patient with my young son. I would often drift away in a train of negative thinking. I would sit at home in silence doing nothing, just getting lost in the nothingness of my mind. I would go to bed early and just cry. Days would go by, and though I tried to keep my positive attitude and joyful spirit intact, the thoughts kept coming back.

This exercise of letting negative thoughts go is harder to execute than some will have you think. How exactly can one find the strength to want to let go of these fears if one knows that they might come right back? I am at a place now where I can make peace with the fact that I am bound to have these moments of craze and anxiety on occasion. However, the difference now is that I am able to recognize the triggers, work through the emotions that take hold for a minute, and breathe them out ... Winning every time feels like winning over a part of myself that can be fearful.

It has been a few years since the main trigger of my anxiety appeared. Following the stress of my divorce and the multitude of adjustments to my daily routine as a single mother of a young child, I was feeling lost. Seven years later, I continue to make strides in the way that I manage my anxiety. I've won the battle, and I've become a project manager to my symptoms. I continuously evaluate tools and practices that are available to help keep symptoms away. Among my allies: meditation and breathing techniques. The one idea that I find so difficult but that is key to winning over anxiety is facing our fears. In her book *Living Well with Anxiety*, Carolyn Chambers Clark shares her approach to dealing successfully with anxiety:

"Although you may want to escape from uncomfortable feelings or fight them, you can achieve even more control by inviting the symptoms."

I used to think that the last thing I wanted to do was to make an inventory of the thoughts or things or situations that make me feel anxious and to voluntarily go there. But, as time has gone by and I have become more comfortable with this exercise, I make it a habit. When I get tense inside, when I feel overwhelmed by emotions, I take a deep breath and I think about the most dreadful ideas in that very moment. Then I ask myself, "What is my greatest fear? What is the worst that can happen?"

Dealing with my fears is an old practice for me, you know. I tried to tackle this situation a long time ago without much success. I've read books about self-improvement and I've listened to thousands of hours of my favorite speakers on the subject of mindfulness. I've meditated to the deep messages of Deepak Chopra and I've listened to religious leaders address the human condition and its many lessons. For me, this business of facing my fears is directly connected to the ability of staying present.

"Okay fear, what now?"

By now, I've mastered the practice of inviting fearful thoughts into my life. The self-exploration goes something like this:

⚙ Is it the fear of being alone? This one I've felt for a long time. But when you are alone, you find out about things that you didn't know before. You have space to be by yourself, and maybe this is the season for it. Also, being alone is not the same as being lonely.

⚙ Is it the fear of losing my job? Yes, I've been there, like millions of other Americans. You pretty much go through it, and eventually, another opportunity, another door opens, and you move on.

⚙ Is it a fear of not being smart enough in my current job? Well, I've gone pretty far so far in my life. I look around and I realize that I'm in a fairly good place. I have many blessings that I feel grateful for; therefore, I must be doing something right.

Then I move to other thoughts: Am I afraid of not being a good enough mom for my child? Aha, we are getting closer to that sticky area of balancing a job and a personal life. As a single mom, dealing with this fear is especially tricky and sensitive, because there is a lot of guilt attached to it … but deal with it I must. I go down the list and I'm pretty much exhausted from the exercise. For how long do I need to do this? I wonder. Luckily, I don't need to torture myself every day with this exercise.

Dealing with fear is not a "one shot deal" and boom, your fear is gone. There is no pill that can help you get rid of your fears, at least not permanently. Dealing with fear is an ongoing practice. It's like waking up every morning and having the same routine. It's something that I've had to learn to live with—and expect to have in my life. Sometimes it appears as candlelight, other times like a savage wildfire that threatens to take over my life experience. On any given day, I'm as happy as a clam. I love the mornings, especially, but sometimes along the day the creepy uneasy feelings that follow the thoughts of fear want to take hold.

"You are not alone." The sound of my voice seemed to have come from someone else.

On the evening of that Easter, I found myself giving my friend Christine a warm hug. Christine is a young psychologist that treats highly depressed individuals who are in desperate need of therapy. Her job can be extremely overwhelming sometimes. Offering counsel and listening to the stories of those who suffer from severe depression can be a huge challenge, even for the bravest of therapists. On that evening, she and I were joined in the feeling of being brave against the anxiety in others, and in my case, in myself.

NOTHING THAT YOU FEAR IS REAL

What I learned through the process of identifying my fears and inviting them into my awareness is that I was making up the stories that made me afraid. It was not a given that I was unequipped to be a working mom who could balance motherhood and work. It was a made-up story that would tell me I couldn't do a good job at both. Granted, the struggles that come with working and being a mom are real, and if you ask stay-at-home moms what it's like to balance their daily chores,

I'm sure they will tell you that it's hard to take care of a home and also retain their independence as woman. I've had friends who longed for a time when they could leave the home to join a group of adults in serious conversations that are not related to the schoolwork or after-school activities of their children.

I barely survived that Easter Sunday, but I emerged stronger and all the more clear about the triggers that can cause my anxiety. I got home and found comfort in my bed, the smell of lavender and vanilla from a soothing candle by my side. I revisited the moment when I had said my goodbyes earlier that evening. I had hugged my family and whispered words that I repeat to myself in moments when I feel the most despair: You are not alone.

3

Connecting with My Son

Tell me and I'll forget. Show me and I'll remember.
Involve me and I'll understand.

— Confucius

As a first-time parent, I didn't know what to expect. The parenting books that I read and the advice that I got from others could only help so much. I hoped that I'd be the best parent I could be. As much as I prepared to provide for the main responsibilities—nutrition, safety, and nurturing of my son's mind and spirit—I never considered an important aspect of parenting: how to communicate effectively with my child. I thought that the mother instinct would lead me, that I'd be able to easily perceive what my child's moods meant, and that I'd be able to tell how he was feeling at all times. I assumed that creating a meaningful connection with my child would come naturally.

I spent years in college learning about how to be an excellent communicator; therefore, when I became a mother I thought that communicating with my son Lucian would be a "piece of cake." When he was a baby there was only me doing the talking, so that part was easy. As he grew older and was able to speak, it would be more challenging to make sure that he would understand what I needed from him. Looking back, I see I must have been mostly having one-way conversations with him, especially when I was tired or stressed. On those days, I would talk without really listening to the response that I was getting.

As Lucian grew older, he became very much aware of things that he didn't like about my style of communicating with him. As a toddler, he would readily voice his disapproval of my ways. I would listen and then I'd think about what he was really trying to tell me. I can blame my anxiety for the many times when my communication with my child wasn't the most effective. If I raised my voice, Lucian would close up. I would revert to my lower tone again, but soon after, I would go back to my "high" tone of voice.

Some cultures are used to interactions where the tone of voice is lively, the hands are in the air, the body is moving; conversations are enhanced with examples and stories are illustrated with gestures. In Puerto Rico, this type of interaction is the norm.

At their core, effective communication skills with children are not different from those used in communication with adults. Below are the four basic steps of any effective conversation:

1. Issue your message
2. Listen attentively
3. Establish empathy
4. Respond accordingly

Since he was born, I'd thought I would excel at communicating with Lucian. I was obsessed about "connecting" with him in such a way that he could understand not just what I was trying to say but the feelings behind my words.

With time, as I've searched for a true connection beyond the casual exchange with Lucian, I've had to face the fact that my anxiety can undermine my best intentions to communicate effectively, to connect at a deeper level with him.

There are many definitions for the word "connection." Here is my favorite, from author Dr. Brené Brown:

> *Connection is the energy that exists between people when they feel seen, heard, and valued; when they can give and receive without judgement; and when they derive sustenance and strength from the relationship.*

In my eight years as a mother to my son Lucian, our connection has been strong at times, but very poor at others. When he was a toddler, for example, I used to struggle with some behaviors of his that I felt might be coming from a place of belligerence or defiance. In those moments when I'm not connecting with my son, I have been blinded by the emotions of the moment and by the need to control the situation.

When I was in the midst of the anxiety-ridden stage, as I like to call it, not only did I have poor communication with my son, but also I would unleash my anger modes, often with very little self-control.

"Don't spank him like that, Ada!" my mom said one gloomy afternoon as she shook her head, looking at me with sad eyes, almost on the brink of tears. She had witnessed her daughter violently slapping the legs of her two-year-old grandson. I remember that day clearly. My mom was visiting for a few days and we had gone shopping. Lucian was refusing to sit in the car seat and I couldn't get him to be still. His tiny legs kicking in the air, his arms up, he would not let me get the straps around his legs. He wanted out. The problem is that Lucian always wanted out of the car seat. Regardless of the situation, whether we were leaving home or his daycare, seven out of ten times, and from the ages of one and a half to three years, the little boy refused to sit quietly and willingly in the car seat. As I sat in the driver's seat and drove away, I felt a sinking feeling inside.

I know all about spanking. I had my share when I was a kid. My mom had no business reprimanding me on this one. Not because she can't call out the things that she disagrees with, but in this case I had learned from her example. I think she knew then, as she knows now, that I was doing my best.

Nowadays, I reflect on the days when I used to spank Lucian and I feel sad, yet I feel a lot of compassion for myself. I never was one to spank Lucian often, but I wish I'd never felt that I had to. I realize that my temper went "over the top" because of a combination of stress, worries, and a young child who was strong-willed.

Tantrums aside, I was also dealing with Lucian's constant refusal to wear most types of clothing because of his eczema. I had never heard about eczema before I had Lucian. When he was a baby, he would cry incessantly and scratch his arms and legs. I couldn't figure out why he was itching so badly. We tried all kinds of ointments and skin lotions, to no avail. I used to have him wear mittens all the time. One evening he was scratching so bad he bled. I learned to have the right lotions ready at hand whenever he would start scratching. Flare-ups appear during the change of seasons when his skin gets very dry, or when he is exposed to allergens in the environment or on clothing. Getting my boy ready in the mornings was the most dreadful thing for me. I knew the minute I put those pants on him, he would scream and kick or somehow complain. It has taken a lot of time and patience, not only to discover where to find the clothes that don't make him feel uncomfortable, but also to get the appropriate medicated lotions to treat his eczema.

Getting the right clothes for Lucian over the years has been a challenge. While other moms normally grab clothes and go, I've had to buy various options and keep the receipt because I never knew if Lucian would agree to wear the clothes. Sometimes he would seem agreeable, and then on the day that I would lay them out for him to wear, he would throw a fit. It's yet another source of stress which has put my son and me at odds on a regular basis.

It's not because he means to be difficult. This I've learned the hard way. His dry skin and eczema can turn into hives, or he can simply get random rashes anywhere. His extreme sensitivity to most fabrics can drive me insane every time I attempt to get him to wear "proper" clothes rather than the regular "athletic clothes" that he prefers to wear. As he has gotten older, instead of throwing a tantrum, he will voice his disagreement over what I put in front of him. Any fabric that feels too rough or too tight against his skin is the cause of a long argument.

"Why did you buy this shirt? It's itchy!"

Finding the perfect size in shirts and pants for Lucian can also be a challenge. If it's too loose in his waist it's annoying, if it's too tight under his arms he doesn't like it, and if the material is too thick it makes him hot. Cotton button-down shirts? Not happening. He refuses to wear anything that is buttoned down because it "scratches" his skin. Jeans with a zipper? Not a chance. It's too hard to close them at the top.

Over the years, I've learned to be more mindful in my approach to dealing with his discomfort over certain clothing. Instead of pulling out one option, I lay out two options, and when he complains about a set of clothes, I try to let go of my need to choose for him and let him choose for himself. I've learned to go with the flow. Clothing shouldn't be something to get exasperated about. For this anxious mom, the battles over which clothes Lucian will wear have been many. I know I'll miss the day when he no longer needs me to put some lotion on his back or on his legs after he showers in the evening or in the mornings. The boy is growing and slowly he is letting go of things that he needed mom to do for him—which can relieve many stressors in my anxiety-o-meter. Kudos for growing up.

In the meantime, while Lucian is still a child I make every attempt to be more mindful in my communication with him. When I pick him up from school, I look him in the eyes and make sure that I am connecting with him. If I'm driving, I listen attentively. I turn the music off and I ask him about his day. I wait, because the true feelings often don't come out in his first comment. It normally takes a few minutes before Lucian gets comfortable and starts sharing his thoughts about the day. I am patient; I wait until the most significant revelations come out of my little boy's heart. Often he wants to share about what happened with a friend at school. Many times his stories have a quick end. However, there are times when Lucian goes on and on. He tells me about an argument with a friend, or an accident that happened when he was playing during recess. I'm driving, but I'm listening. I can sense that Lucian feels a sense of relief when he shares his stories with me.

Becoming more mindful about my communication with my son has made me adjust the basic steps of communication that I learned in college. I've slowly evolved in my intention to connect with my child and therefore I've adapted the way that I used to communicate with him to incorporate a more mindful approach to our conversations:

> B ~ Become aware
>
> R ~ Release existing modes
>
> E ~ Express how you are feeling
>
> A ~ Adapt your message
>
> T ~ Talk with your child, not at your child
>
> H ~ Hold your child tenderly
>
> E ~ Evaluate

This approach to communicating with our children involves coming into a conversation with an intention. It also implies the idea that we are coming to a conversation to "be" with our child rather than to "tell" something to our child. Therefore, "being" becomes a priority in our interaction.

Mindful conversations happen anytime between me and my son. These days, our conversations can be short or long. However, what's different from the old way of communicating with my child is that I now allow for more flexibility on my part. I come to the conversation with the mindset of listening, and also of learning about my son. An implied question can be "How is he doing? How is his spirit doing today?"

Conversations sometimes end abruptly. When we arrive home from school, for example, Lucian jumps quickly out of the car and goes inside, hungry or ready to turn the TV on. I know it's his time to relax. I know that I'll be looking for the next moment to connect with him again, which is usually at night, when we cuddle to read a book.

As Lucian has gotten older and better at expressing his needs, his desires and his feelings, I have become more aware of my role in his life. I can be more respectful of his space, for example, because he can let me know when he wants a break from the noise in our environment. Sometimes when we are in the car, he asks me to turn the radio off, and I realize he is not a baby anymore, and I also realize that the silence I sometimes crave is also helpful for Lucian. At the same time, I've become open to new ideas, to new ways of understanding our mother-and-child relationship. I feel as if we've reached a point where we understand each other completely. Our communication is more open and we are calm in our daily interactions. The feeling that I am able to reach into my son's soul and truly connect with him is priceless.

LOVE THE JOB

Learning what my talents are and where they are best utilized has shown me new ideas, and places where I feel that I can both like what I do and feel connected to the mission that I'm supporting as a professional. I realize there is a part of me that wants to control where my career is going. With time, however, and years of experience under my belt, I've learned to respect the path that life has presented to me.

In terms of my level of anxiety, I must admit that having a job that is fulfilling, and where I feel that I'm being challenged, has played a role in my keeping a positive outlook and energy. When things in my job have changed and the environment has turned less than exciting, I've become disappointed and some-times hopeless. The dreamer in me wants to be excited every day at my contributions to the world. The years when I was im-mersed in the turmoil of anxiety, I would feel that the ground was shaking under my feet. Things didn't seem to be going the way I wanted them to go. During those times, I remember thinking that I had good intentions, and while I'd see the bright side of things, sometimes darkness could come and slip in.

It would take me a long time to respect the divine timing of things. Let me explain what I'm referring to when I talk about divine timing with regard to my job:

The best of intentions had kept me working hard at my job, but I could sense I no longer belonged in that beautiful place. It had been a beautiful place for over 13 years, but, in-creasingly, every day at the CNN Center started to feel like a drag: the normalcy of breaking news that can break anyone's trust in humans displayed in monitors for the world to see, the hard work of those trying to bring the truth behind politics, the nuisance of how stories make it to light, the stories behind the stories, the reporters that risk their lives to deliver the news, the ungrateful masses who watch in disbelief, the small population that increasingly finds other outlets for information, the paradox of selling news programs that will depress a whole nation. The irony of those who want to tell the best of stories but are strapped with limitations imposed by budgets, logistics, security issues and politics.

A job that I adored and that I enjoyed so much for such a long time had me delivering communication products that carried, in my view, honest and trustworthy information that would be consumed by business and political leaders across the world. Information that, when used correctly, would help them make decisions as they shaped their companies, their communities, their countries. Information that could help ensure that democracy continued to find a home in remote lands. It was an important job. Through marketing and publicity, I promoted news content that I found valuable, except the daily tasks didn't feel as exciting anymore. Changes in the industry and the looming waves of structural changes in the company, combined with the very poignant nature of the affairs that the news network was covering, were all affecting me at a deeper level. I could never have suspected that after many years on the job, things would start to feel different. Even the stories that we were working on began to have an unwanted effect on me.

One time, in late 2012, I was working on the promotion of an upcoming documentary. Filmed in the Middle East and in Asia, the production would tell the story of a young boy who was attacked by a street gang, beaten and mutilated. He was left in a ditch and found later by his father, who miraculously brought him to safety. I've thought often of this boy, hoping that he is growing up in a safe environment. For what he endured, he is my hero. I can't write all the details of this story—its impact has been that profound.

I sat in my office with a print copy of the preliminary script of the documentary in my hands. In advance of our marketing communication program planning, I'd read about the details of the story to understand what the report was going to be about so that our team could develop a plan for our promotions on the field, across Latin America. I was perplexed, immobilized by the cruelty of these men, and I was terribly sad about what had happened to this child. I thought about my own child, and the overthinking mode started to play with my mind.

"I can't," I said to myself as I walked across the hall, my eyes welling up when I entered my boss's office a few minutes later.

I only said a few words but she understood exactly where I was coming from. She knew too well the heaviness that comes with reading "hard" news every day. After a while, you have to develop a thick skin. I walked back to my office feeling a little better after that quick chat, but it was still very hard to understand the brutality of this story. It wasn't the easiest of stories to work with, but I had a job to do. A few short months later, I bid farewell to my "alma mater," CNN. The memories of my good intentions clashed with the awkwardness of the last months on the job that I knew I wasn't connecting with anymore, my respect for the men and women who do one of the hardest jobs on the planet, every day, without seeking money or fame. From Mexico to Iraq, there are countries where journalists are targeted by criminals, often killed, because of the stories that they are trying to uncover. I will forever cherish the honor of having worked with them, and for them.

Lucian was four when we made the decision to enroll him in a wonderful school about 20 minutes from home. We were looking at pre-K programs, and my friend Elizabeth had enrolled her son, who is the same age as Lucian. I couldn't have been more excited. I had started a new job at a D.C.-based nonprofit that manages contracts for the CDC, and changing jobs brought, as I expected, work in the area of government contracts and health communications, and many exciting projects. There was a lot of learning for me in a new area of communications, and I welcomed the challenge.

The new job afforded a more flexible schedule, a laid-back office environment, and a more mom-friendly routine. However, just when I felt that my stress would diminish, I began suffering from what I'd call "random" health issues that turned my life upside down for a very long time.

It was the fall of 2014, and after suffering from mild sinus infections, I had been prescribed antibiotics three or four times within six months, without any probiotics to go along with the medication. Though I had suffered "feminine infections" in the past, this time I started developing recurring episodes with very painful symptoms that would last for days, even after the feminine infections were cleared. If you are a mom, you know what that feels like. If you've never had one, trust me, you don't want one. Imagine having one after the other for months. I'd go see my doctor and they'd recommend the typical antifungal, and a week later I'd be back again in their office with the same symptoms.

"What in the world is happening to my health? What's wrong with my body?" I said to myself on those gloomy days.

Timing aside, the divine plan would bring a new challenge that I had to be open to accepting. It wasn't an easy one, and I know now that millions of women can understand how anxiety can also affect us when we are suffering from an illness or a disease. Around the time that I changed jobs, I started feeling sick, and I was sick for a long time. The name of my condition? Candidiasis.

THE GIFTS OF CANDIDA

"Go eat, Ada," said the voice of a lady that to this day I think of as Cruella from Disney's *101 Dalmatians*. I'd had a long day at work and I was exhausted. She had flown in from New York and was only visiting our office on this one occasion, yet to this day I remember how unkind her comment was. I was so thin, though. Exactly 105 pounds thin. Surely she hadn't meant to sound that mean, but she did, and it only added to my current state of anxiety.

It took me almost three years to rid myself of candidiasis, and a few deep meditation sessions to forgive Cruella for her demeaning commentary. If you haven't heard of candidiasis, or candida, as it's called informally, you are not the only one. An immune system disease that is not widely recognized by physicians, it's defined by blogs and online articles everywhere as the "overgrowth of yeast in your digestive tract." A "fungus" is a microscopic organism that lives in our bodies without causing issues; however, when it overgrows it affects the immune system. In my case, I feel that it was the overuse of antibiotics to treat sinus infections in 2014 that caused this overgrowth in my digestive tract. The symptoms vary from abdominal pain and fatigue to bloating and yeast-like infections. Candida has been called a "largely unknown epidemic" in the United States because it affects so many; yet because the symptoms are similar to other disorders, it is very hard to diagnose. There is not a single shot treatment that can cure candida, but the disorder requires that you change your diet drastically to eliminate sugars and other products that feed the fungus.

Candidiasis had knocked on my door and had decided to let herself in. I thought I had never heard the word "candidiasis" before but then I remembered that my Aunt Estella had suffered from something similar. She provided a lot of helpful advice throughout that time. For almost three years I had to endure a different kind of living, one that would require that I give up some of my favorite meals. In order to beat candida, I had to follow a very strict diet without sugars, pasta, milk, bread … especially bread. I couldn't have any pastry, and I was not allowed to have wine.

Standing in front of the ice cream section at the grocery store I would want to grab the meanest, fanciest, most delicious pint that I could find. The problem? All of them had sugar, and the ones that didn't tasted like … well, those tasted okay. In the absence of bread, I used to feel that I should be able to at least have a spoonful my favorite ice cream.

Suffering from candida caused an interesting dynamic with Lucian. Not all of it terribly painful, luckily, and with both positives and negatives. It was so hard cooking the most delicious meals full of yummy things that children like, such as cheese, sauces, creams, and bread, and having to watch as my son, who has an amazing talent for wiping things off his plate in no time, ate things that I was not able to touch for fear of getting so sick to my stomach that I would have to go straight to bed. Baby showers, I'd skip. Wine-tasting (my favorite!)? Out of the question. My weekends became nothing but a reminder that I couldn't have as much fun as I used to—in more areas than one. I was in lockdown mode, with a book in my hand or watching movies without a bowl of ice cream. The best that I could do was eat a couple of plain almonds with a cup of chamomile tea. Have at it, Ada.

Yet, candida brought about major lessons for this non-believer in dieting. I have been blessed with a fast metabolism and had never experienced strict dieting. In fact, the closest to dieting I had come was when I was trying to lose weight after my pregnancy, and even then I lost the baby weight rather quickly. However, after I began suffering from candida, my favorite foods were prohibited, and the most festive of affairs would remind me that I was (a) mega skinny and (b) not able to have a full meal. I have a lot of respect for those who have suffered from candida. I'm a survivor of this crazy thing, and to this day I have to watch my intake of certain sugars, otherwise I will have a setback. And even after all these years, my body still reminds me that I'll fare better if I stay away from sugar.

On the other hand, I became such a smart eater after my candida crisis. Candida made me a wiser shopper and a smarter mom in the kitchen. I look at the labels of products like a spy; the amount of sugar doesn't paint the whole picture: anything that ends in "gum" and anything that seems like a word your mother would not have used falls into that category. Yet the challenge of finding organic food that I can eat has made me more conscious of the ingredients in the food that my son eats.

"No vegetables, no dessert." I have laid down the rule and Lucian knows that he must comply, otherwise he won't get "benefits." Benefits in my home mean a sweet dessert or access to technology. The threat saves my day.

Insisting that my child eat vegetables used to cause me stress. I remember the organic meals that I used to eat when I was a child. Fresh chicken was easily found in the nearest supermarket and fresh eggs from the hens that my mom had gotten for us.

Some things are easy to let go—thoughts that are negative or habits that you know you can easily change. However, there are things that can be a bit more challenging to let go. Should I insist on having my child eat his vegetables? Should I insist on setting a timer for my son's use of electronics? Should I insist on asking that my son tuck his shirt inside his pants or wear a belt every day? All those questions would come frequently to the mind of this anxious mom. Yet, I've learned to choose which questions to pay attention to.

In those days I would choose my battles. As mothers, I know that we are all trying our best, but I've learned to catch myself when I'm going down the route of arguing with my son over things that ultimately are trivial. Controlling the situation was for many years my way of exerting power over my child. When I was in that mode, I was hiding from a deeper truth. Sometimes the arguments were valid, sometimes I had to be consistent in my enforcement of rules. Other times, however, my angry reactions over simple things had more to do with my own feelings and emotions than the need to discipline my child.

Our own unhappiness, our own feelings of unfulfillment in our job or at home, or a debilitating disease can make us feel that we must control the little things that we are able to. Sometimes the pain that we inflict on our children when we are too busy comes from a place of feeling that we don't have control of our lives.

WHO AM I TO JUDGE?

Does that phrase sound familiar? These five words were said a few years ago by Pope Francis when he candidly answered a question from a journalist regarding his views about acceptance of homosexuals in the Catholic Church. Judging was a favorite pastime of my mind. While it never amused me to hurt others with my opinions, I have to admit that I spent years trying to be the perfect professional, the perfect friend, the perfect wife; and along the way, I had very high standards for how things should be done.

It was after reading the book *The Power of Now* by Eckhart Tolle that I made a conscious effort to let things be and not judge. It was way before I became I mom, and what I learned has served me well in my mom duties. By not judging, we acknowledge the fact that we don't know everything, and that we don't have the moral authority to tell others how they should live. By trying not to judge, we are also doing ourselves a huge favor. We are letting go of the need to have an opinion about everything, from the trivial things to the ones that might seem transcendental to our human endeavor.

Judging becomes a way of being. We transfer this judging to our homes and become dictators around the house. Sometimes we get carried away by the emotions of the moment, light or heavy as they might be, and when we are in a stressed state, we might expect that our children act according to our demands, most, if not all, of the time. From the color of the shirt he chooses in the morning to the way he combs his hair, I have found myself judging everything about my child, and I have to stop myself because it is exhausting.

It was February of 2015 and I was going on a date night with a girlfriend. We were headed to a concert of *The Producers* in downtown Atlanta and, beforehand, we stopped for pizza at a local restaurant. With my friend were her husband and their adorable son. As we enjoyed our pizza, we started chatting about school events and about some children who might be leaving school because they were moving out of the area. As moms, we exchanged ideas and were happy to see our boys make good friendships at school. It was a regular conversation where sometimes one makes comments about other parents. The typical gossip moment that moms can sometimes have a hard time avoiding showed up that night during our conversation over pizza: the "I know better than they do," type of conversation. Fortunately, it was a short exchange, yet I couldn't help my anxious mind going away with my opinion.

"Do not judge, my friend," I said.

"Oh, I'm not judging."

My friend understood what I meant, and my advice fortunately was well received. My friend's husband, who was sitting across the table, smiled at our friendly exchange. We agreed to disagree at one point, then we completely agreed over other ideas shared during our lively conversation. I love it when two smart girlfriends can politely share their views but are able to disagree. Sometimes there is a wise man in the background who decides that it is best to sit quietly and listen to what the ladies have to say.

My comment to my friend stemmed from a practice that I've adopted which has helped me deal with my anxiety. "Do not feel that you have to judge everything." This particular advice comes from an experienced, now-retired "judge-everything" specialist.

I used to have an opinion about everyone and everything. I was pretty outspoken and still am, yet nowadays, I try to *stop* having the need to have an opinion on things. If my neighbor planted flowers and I don't exactly like the way they look, I let it be. If my mother calls to let me know she plans to buy a new car that I don't like for her, or to let me know she is going to give money away to her church, I let her do what she thinks is best. I like to tell my friends, "If your husband decides to spend his afternoon working on his car or motorcycle instead of joining you and the kids for ice cream, give the man a break." Don't feel that you need to impose your views on every aspect of your family's life. Don't feel that you need to change things and make people around you agree with you to feel validated.

This doesn't mean that as a mother and a wife you don't have a right to ask for what you need or express your feelings in a relationship. What I'm suggesting here is to take a step back and watch for triggers that could cause tension and anxiety in the relationship with a spouse. Sometimes those tensions can spill over and spoil the calmness that you want to create around your children.

I realize that our minds are active, we are smart and opinionated at times, and we've earned the right to be heard. The school of life has given mothers and working mothers alike plenty of lessons to learn, and as women we are ready to impart lectures that will solidify what we know best.

I'm not suggesting that one shouldn't give an opinion about matters that they care deeply about. What I'm saying is, let's try to have a more relaxed state of mind about things around us. Let things flow a bit and ride the wave of life, so to speak. You'll find that you will be removing quite a load from your shoulders.

"Mom, where are my shorts?"

When Lucian was seven he declared that he didn't want to wear long pants to school because, according to him, they felt uncomfortable. The anxious mom in me was not having it. I went into dictator mode. One morning, not long after the series of arguments over Lucian's refusal to wear long pants, I was browsing the Web and stumbled upon a blog that talked about the launch of a brand of children's clothing which was specifically designed for children who have sensitivity to certain fabrics. I wondered if my son's issues were extreme or if it was a phase that would soon pass. I decided that maybe I shouldn't insist so much about this whole idea that wearing long pants during colder months was a must. I let it go.

About six months later, without my insisting on his wearing either type of pants, my son announced that he wanted to wear long pants. He had realized that he could protect his legs not only from the cold weather but also from getting scratches he when he played outside. I'm now able to just let things be; I have to *let him be*.

I wish I had heard this advice more often when my son was younger: "This stage where the child is right now will soon pass." Which means stay the course, because the circumstances that are happening now will soon fade. As children get older, they become more mature, and in my case, my child became more easygoing. I've struggled with the clothes situation for so long, yet lately Lucian wears his belt without complaining. There is light!

THE BEAUTY OF SLEEPTIME

The article in the glossy lifestyle magazine that I was reading talked about the beauty secrets of Hollywood stars who are of a certain age. One of them declared that her secret to looking beautiful was sleeping at least eight to nine hours every night. My reaction was "I wish." Who can afford to sleep eight hours every night? Not most of the moms that I know. Between cleaning the kitchen after dinner and putting the children down to bed, there are not enough hours in the day, let alone the night.

I should stop here talking about my everlasting love for sleep. Ever since I was a kid, I just loved napping as much as I could. I napped everywhere—between classes or in the afternoon, after lunch in the car outside in a parking lot or at the beach, and on the weekends. Some moms can operate with very little sleep, but me, if I'm not rested enough I'll have very little patience to handle the next day like a normal person. I know it affects how patient I can be. But the lack of sleep doesn't just affect moms; children also need their beauty rest.

There is plenty of research that shows that in our current society children don't get to sleep enough, and I'm here to confirm that some of us are better off sleeping beyond eight hours every night. By the time we get home on weekdays, it's easily past 6:00 p.m. A conversation around the table during dinner is squeezed in, and more often than not the TV is sounding in the background. Then it's time to finish homework and head to the bathroom for the nightly routine.

For children under the age of eight, mothers might still be reading a book before the lights are turned down, and what an important practice this is in the development of children. The images in children's books are so fantastic. When I read out loud, I'm taking the place of the narrator and I'm also being, in a way, a child again.

The playful side of me comes out every night, and I know why Lucian looks forward to this special time with me. I ask him, "What book do you want to read tonight, Sweetie?" And when I'm reading to Lucian at night, I'm consciously calming myself down. I can show my child a calmer side, speak to him in a lower tone of voice, and be the momma bear that every child wants.

We should do a better job of promoting the importance of reading to our children. Beyond the obvious benefits that instilling a love of reading brings to succeeding in life, I feel it is a unique time to get closer to my child, physically but also emotionally. Lucian loves it when I sit next to him and we snuggle to read a book. At times when I've been too tired, he's been the one to say, "No book, Mommy?" I make the effort. I put a pause to my thought trains and remember the importance of being there for my child at a time when we can connect on a deeper level.

On a typical night, soon after we read the books, I would lie down next to Lucian until he fell asleep. Some days he had a hard time falling asleep, so I tried to get us both relaxed with breathing exercises. I took deep breaths and started to count out loud so that Lucian could follow: one, two, three. I reflected on the day's adventures and tried to help him move past his fears.

Knowing that absolutely nothing of what I fear is real, I realize it's just an idea that my imagination has created, and that has empowered me in so many ways. But what if the fear that you are feeling is real? That's when the practice of silence comes in handy.

I've slowly gained a knack for striking up conversations with moms like me. I can sense working moms who are juggling many things at a time, some more anxious than others.

I want to talk to them, let them know that they are not alone. Some seem very chatty and outspoken, some very introverted about challenges in their lives. It's not that easy to spot an anxious mom like me, because while I can be chatty, I reserve my freak-out moments and concerns for myself. There is a fear of disapproval, of course. I have my moments of being outspoken, as in, "I don't give a damn, I admit it, I need help!" And I also have a more serene, introverted way of being, as if saying quietly, "I don't want anyone to find out how really, very stressed-out-of-my-mind I mostly am." For the most part, however, I walk alone with the blocks on my back and the lines in my forehead.

Really, any way you look at it, as an anxious mom I recognize that there are times when one could be more calm, more serene. It is then when we should do more of a very important thing: invite more spaces of silence into our lives.

Quieting my mind and my body has helped me cope with the feelings of anxiety. I remember the first time I tried to meditate, sitting there with my eyes closed without saying a word. It felt like an impossible task to be quiet for three minutes, not to mention the recommended fifteen to twenty minutes a day that yogis advocate for a healthy lifestyle. Quieting my mind was challenging at first, but once I practiced a few times and got in the habit of staying still for a few minutes, I noticed that it helped me feel more relaxed throughout the day. The easiest way for me to invite silence into my daily routine is by playing a meditation audio. I keep a collection of meditation series that I listen to at least four or five times a week, and I credit this practice, along with a healthy diet, regular exercise, and at least eight hours of sleep, with helping me to feel better and have a better handle on my anxiety.

Before going to bed, I run through the list of all the things that I have to accomplish the next day. Sure, I have the calendar on my cell phone up to date, but the reminder of this list of things that need to happen—some of them completely out of my circle of influence—can keep me up at night. I end up tossing and turning. I play a meditation video of my favorite spiritual guru until I eventually fall asleep. The extent of my concerns is not limited to my ability to get my son to school on time or get myself to work on time. There is that project that my son has to turn in and the book report that he will be presenting that can keep me up. I wonder if he will feel at ease, if the words will flow, if he will be okay. I wake up and the crazy routine begins, just like for millions of other parents around the world. As a single mom, the stress of getting things ready for the day can be daunting, but as my wise mother has reminded me in countless phone conversations through the years since my divorce, preparation and anticipation can be my best allies. I know that I'm not alone; for the married spouse with the husband traveling the world, the stress of balancing life can be daunting. Yet by adopting the habit of anticipation and preparation, we can help alleviate the symptoms of stress that can erupt at home.

My brain works differently, I think, because I think about the same thing again and again. I was officially diagnosed with mild anxiety only recently and instead of feeling terribly sad, I remember feeling a sense of relief. Why, you might ask? For me it was a confirmation that something about the way I thought about things was a bit off and there was a *reason* why I was feeling a bit off. My closest friends might have been able to notice because of my pattern of overthinking things, obsessing over events or experiences that might happen.

How does one get to be anxious enough to be diagnosed with anxiety? I've started to analyze the early years of my life and how anxiety might have been present all along, without my noticing. I was always a talkative child, and "hyperactive" is a term that teachers would use to describe me. Sitting still wasn't too easy for me. One of my legs would always be shaking under the table. Other than that, I would not have considered myself an "anxious" person.

My doctor explained how certain circumstances in my life were leading me toward anxiety. In his view, the fact that I was suffering from anxiety made sense, because at that time I was going through a series of difficult circumstances. A single mom, I had lost my job around that time, so the stress of balancing work and my personal life would very understandably cause me to be stressed. Aside from this, I could sense that over the past few years, since my divorce, my level of anxiety had slowly increased. Of course I would never have identified this on my own.

Having anxiety, even if mild, meant that I could now explain why I felt the way I was feeling lately: the feeling of being overwhelmed and the lack of sleep at times, the feeling of being rushed from the inside out. I am a functioning anxious woman, but still, I had felt this for some time and now I could give it a name.

If anxiety happens when certain chemicals in the brain are not communicating correctly, what then can I do to fix this? Beyond taking medication, what else could I do? I thought. Defined as a feeling of worry, unease, or fearfulness, anxiety is an experience unique to human beings. Whatever the cause, it seems that when a person perceives an imminent danger, the reaction of his/her body can cause tension, restlessness, and angst.

If you met me at work or at my son's school or at church during the weekend, you would never suspect that I struggle with anxiety, but I do. As I navigate the spaces of motherhood, and balance my life as a mom with the life of a professional, and then add my family and friends, I can tell you I'm managing well. Not perfectly, but well.

When I was diagnosed with mild generalized anxiety, the doctor recommended that I read about the condition. He gave me a long list of books and explained that there are very different types of anxiety. As I read more about the topic, I started to understand the complexity of anxiety as a disease, and that identifying which type of anxiety a person is suffering from might not be easy. Perhaps this is one of the reasons why so many mental health issues are hard to diagnose by general physicians. One person can show symptoms that are easily identified as signs of anxiety, while another can show a combination of symptoms that can point to more than one condition and that may or may not include anxiety. Symptoms of anxiety are such that they can lead a general physician to confuse it with depression, for example. Experts have identified different types of anxiety, and as I recently learned, women are more likely to suffer from the very type that I've experienced: generalized anxiety. Also known as GAD (generalized anxiety disorder), this is the anxiety that causes a person to feel worried or afraid for several reasons.

As with many physiological ailments, anxiety often begins when a signal in your brain is out of balance. Adrenaline is released in excess and your body starts to experience an array of symptoms. People might complain of shortness of breath, tense muscles, trouble sleeping, nausea and dizziness. In my case, having trouble sleeping and overthinking things have been the symptoms that I've mostly suffered from. And as I learn more about anxiety, I understand how it all works inside the brain, with a million ideas per minute.

The effects on children are a lot more worrisome. Anxiety causes children to be worried about their homework, how their teachers will react and how their friends will react. A child who suffers from anxiety might show signs not only in their emotional health but also physiologically, and when not treated, children are prone to develop depression and other severe mental health issues that can impair their ability to perform at school and in their social life.

Up until that point, I hadn't really understood the impact that my anxiety could have on my son. I felt sad and guilty, that feeling that mothers have when they realize that they can't really be the perfect mom they wish they could be. I thought to myself that, even if I think my anxiety is mild, it might still have an effect on my young son. We all carry stress that can become a burden to our family.

I started imagining the impact that my words could have on my son, and I remember feeling thankful just to have been made aware of this. I've followed a multi-prong approach to dealing with my anxiety. I thought to myself, I'm lucky to be able to tackle this anxiety problem from the root.

I look at the list of triggers for anxiety provided by my doctor, and there it is again: *fear.* The word that I've known since I was a child, personified in the stories of monsters that could come and scare you in the middle of the night. The word that meant a great deal when I was little, then seemed to disappear until I reached my early twenties. I had moved to a new country and I was establishing myself as a professional in a city where I had very few friends and no family at all. Fear took the shape of self-criticism. It was subtle fear, I discovered years later after doing a self-analysis of the roots of my anxiety. During those years, I was afraid of not being smart enough, or of not fitting into a new environment.

I find fear to be so clever. In fact, we could all learn a little bit from the way fear operates. It slowly takes the shape of you, it resides inside of you and hides in the most unimaginable spaces. Then it waits, and it emerges at the most inconvenient of times. Fear takes the side of everyone else but you. This I've learned over the years when I've tried to fit in to a new city. For even when I was a confident youngster, fear could still creep in. I was fun and eloquent in my home country of Puerto Rico, but was I as fun and eloquent in the city of Atlanta? English is my second language and it has been all my life. By Puerto Rican standards, I'm above average in my level of knowledge of the language. However, when I moved to this country, I felt that I had to split my brain in two constantly. Especially because my career demanded that I write in English and Spanish all the time.

The fear of disapproval is something that I'm careful not to pass on to my young son. I tell him often that I love him. I want him to always know that Mom loves him *all* the time, regardless of circumstances. This commitment to loving your child is an innate thing, even to an anxious mom like me. I love my son. Even if we can't always be the best mom in their eyes (especially when we are taking away their electronics as punishment when they misbehave), we are trying our best to love them and to lead the way for them so that they don't have to go through the challenges that we've gone through. And if they must go through the challenges that we had to, then at least we can feel that we've tried our best, that we've given our all to provide them with tools that will help them as they move through life.

4

Within My Soul

The most wasted of all days is one without laughter.

— Nicolas Chamfort

"Mommy, I'm worried," Lucian would say. "Maybe a wolf can get in the house and eat our bunny." I'd reassure Lucian that there were no wolves in our neighborhood and there was no reason to be concerned. "What about a coyote?" he would say. I'd explain how the coyotes couldn't get inside the house. He had heard me talk about coyotes in back of our homes, and that fear just locked inside his head.

I don't remember ever being concerned about a wolf or a coyote eating one of my pets, although when I was around five I saw how a dog violently killed our pet duck. The images have never left me. Luckily, I went on to enjoy many pets, none of them ever being attacked by any animal.

As an anxious mom, I've learned to work through fears by answering questions about situations that make me feel afraid, out of control, or simply overwhelmed:

1. What am I afraid of? What is the event that is causing me to feel scared?
2. Is there an event that I can recall from the past that is causing me physical discomfort?
3. Am I worrying about multiple things, concerns about my health, job or financial security, the health of someone in my family?
4. Am I feeling awkward about a specific situation or a future event?

I've had to answer questions like this in order to better understand my anxiety. I've shared my symptoms with caring physicians who have helped me. Understanding which type of anxiety I suffer from has been helpful, too. Not only have I been able to understand anxiety, but also I'm aware that I have caused anxiety at home, by "spreading" my anxious energy.

Learning more about anxiety has helped me to be understanding when my son has shown tendencies of being worried often, or when he has consistent fears that might be of concern. Having some anxiety is not a bad thing; anxiety keeps us alert, and it helps us better understand some of our most inner feelings. However, when that anxiety is resulting in excessive symptoms, for example lack of sleep, recurring stomach pains or, in chronic cases, an unwillingness to get out of bed, then it should be taken more seriously.

Many things can cause anxiety among children, and each child will present signs of anxiety in a different fashion. Depending of the age of the child, anxiety will affect different areas of their life. In younger children, for example, anxiety can cause sleep problems or a fear of darkness, and it can make older kids insecure in their ability to perform tasks and can cause a lack of concentration at school.

"Now let's focus on your toes, Lucian. Your toes can go to sleep …"

The recording made by Lucian's new friend and therapist, Melanie, put him in a very relaxed state. Starting with the request that Lucian create a force field, Melanie's sweet calming voice would have Lucian picture how his imagination could protect his whole house. The voice asked him to take deep breaths, and he would go deeper into a relaxed state, starting at his toes and then moving on to his calves, bottom, chest, arms, and eventually his back, shoulders, and neck. The recording ended with a gentle reminder that Lucian was loved by Mom and Dad. By then, Lucian would be profoundly asleep.

Lucian has been terrified of being alone at night in his bedroom since he was a toddler. Armed with his light blue fleece blanket and his favorite stuffed animal, my five-year-old Lucian would be ready to fall asleep, but to no avail. I tried everything from keeping the nightlight on to playing soft music, and ultimately I took him to a therapist that could help deal with his fear of being alone at night.

I shared the stories of Lucian's struggles with falling asleep with other moms from his school and was surprised to learn that Lucian's classmates also struggled with fears of being alone in their bedrooms at night. I don't remember having such anxiety myself. As I learn more about how common this is I wonder what other fears Lucian might be feeling through the day when I'm not there to soothe him.

I'm aware that children ages six to nine often experience forms of anxiety such as the fear of being away from their parents. These children feel terribly sad when their parents leave, for instance, on a business trip; they might have trouble with sleeping and eating. They can seem withdrawn and disconnected. The anxious parent, on the other hand, can worry about how their child is adapting to primary school, with disquieting questions like "Is he not feeling good about himself?" or "Is she enjoying going to school?" All of these questions run through my mind as I drop Lucian at his wonderful school in the mornings. I clearly remember his first day in pre-K.

We had been instructed to drop our children at the door, but Lucian wouldn't get out of the car. He was wearing one of my favorite shirts, brown with a truck on the chest. I brought him to the classroom but he wouldn't stay. He followed me out to the hallway, where two teachers met us. As I slowly walked away, resisting the temptation to look back, I could hear his crying and calling me: *"Mo-o-o-mmy!"* I walked down the hallway, and as I turned the corner I saw my little boy sitting, head down, shoulders slumped, the two teachers trying to comfort him.

I took a deep breath and walked away. "He'll be okay," I told myself. And okay he's been since then, most of the time anyway. As he has gotten older, Lucian has displayed different symptoms of what psychologists call "generalized anxiety," which is common in children his age. Fortunately, he is past the stage when he used to feel separation anxiety when I dropped him off at daycare or at pre-K. His fear of being alone at night and his trouble falling asleep have slowly improved over the years.

It was six years since my divorce, and the first time that I had been officially diagnosed with anxiety. In the past I had been prescribed medication to "cope with stress" and with my divorce, but my new doctor recommended that I read a book about anxiety, because he felt I wasn't depressed or stressed; in his view, I was suffering from overthinking patterns. He asked that I read about anxiety, which I felt would be refreshing in a way. It was like categories of anxiousness. Imagine going to a retail store and finding clothes lined up in categories: the sometimes anxious, the always anxious, the super anxious, or the crazy-maniac anxious. I don't think I meant to be funny here, but I had to approach my new diagnosis with some sense of humor.

Just like posttraumatic disorders, we face life challenges without patting ourselves on the back for succeeding at "enduring" a certain stage in our life. No one taught me how to overcome the unexpected death of my dad in a car accident when I was 22, or how to deal with the impact of starting a new life at age 25 in a new city, or how to get through a divorce. These in themselves are circumstances that can create a lot of angst and pain, but also a cumulative effect in anyone. We march on throughout life and we hope to have the tools to deal with things like losing a job, losing a loved one, or losing our home to a natural disaster, some of which are more common than many would think.

Coping mechanisms that are unique to a person will be determined by their own circumstances, and yes, genetics also plays a big role in it. Without getting into the psychological aspects of our own circumstances, which are diverse and complicated, it is clear that most of us walk around with a load that can be buried within our minds. We march on, especially moms, and we pretend that we are fine.

It is difficult to admit that our behavior as adults can negatively affect our children. Who would not want to shield their children from stressful situations? Moving to a new city or school, facing the divorce of parents, or even dealing with the loss of a family member or their pet can lead to great stress in a child's life.

We don't even have to say a word, and those around us might sense that something is bothering us. When a child is exposed to environments of worry and stress, he likely feels less willing to open up and talk about his feelings, for example. When chosen carefully, our words can sound welcoming and tender to our children. Especially when it comes to young children who are learning how to understand the world around them. The words we choose can strengthen and encourage our children, or they can make them feel guilty or shameful.

Family dynamics and genetics can be determining factors in a child's personality and behavior, I've learned. I had my share of issues, I thought. On any given day, my son could be dealing not only with his own frustrations, but also with situations caused by others outside of our home, which in turn could cause him to feel worried. Situations that might not be directly connected to your family, like the death of a friend's family member or news stories that children hear about from others, can cause them extreme worry or concern.

FEELING SAFE

After the infamous school shooting in Orlando early in 2018, my son came home from school with a stick that he had found on the playground.

"Mom, I have an idea."

His idea was that he would build a weapon out of this stick so that he could defend himself and his best buddy in case someone came to the school and tried to hurt them. These are extraordinary times we are living in. Children today experience such an overflow of information. Their little brains have to process and deal with issues that we never even considered when we were growing up.

So, how can I protect my child from dealing with anxiety? How can I prepare my son to deal with the pain that comes from the inevitable series of failures that will meet him at some point or another in his life? As he grows up, he will surely encounter many situations that lead him to experience stressful moments. How will Lucian learn to focus on the positive aspects of his life experience as opposed to the not-so-positive ones? And how can I as a parent help him experience a calm environment that can yield a more peaceful experience at school and at home?

I try to shield Lucian from the news of the day, like the radio shows that recounted how tragic the events were at the Orlando shooting and how students who survived the incident were joining forces with the hope that changes in policy would help protect schools across the nation.

Around this time, we were sitting in the kitchen having dinner when suddenly I came up with what I call a "teachable moment." I might have a teacher inside, because there are times when I enjoy coming up with a theme for Lucian and I to talk about with the intention of making it a moment of learning. I asked the little boy sitting next to me, "Lucian, is the glass half full or half empty?"

He looked at the glass, turned it around, compared it to the glass next to my plate and to the third glass sitting on the table. He was taking his time while I was sweating bullets. I was praying to God and all my angels to please make it so that my son would whisper the two words of wisdom. Meanwhile, my anxious brain was analyzing the possibility that his answer would yield to my deepest disappointment.

I was afraid to know what he would say, this child to whom I've tried to teach the value of appreciating life, of respecting nature, of having compassion, not to mention other invaluable teachings. Would he choose the wrong answer? "Half full, Mom," he finally said. I let out a sigh of relief; I could relax in knowing that my child might have some moments of anxiety, but overall, he was very okay. I was smiling as I looked down at my plate quietly, but inside it was gladness, like a soothing sensation from the corners of my lips to the rest of my body.

The "half-empty" situations in our lives can take over our power to conquer circumstances that are challenging. From feeling uneasy about a situation, children can fall into the trap of "I can't do it." But it's not just children who fall into this trap. Children and adults alike will deal with their feelings of uneasiness when tackling challenges, and feelings of low self-esteem can affect their behavior in different ways.

Fear can manifest in different areas, and many will learn that it is easier to shut down and avoid any situation that can trigger uneasy emotions rather than facing that fear. However, getting children and young adults to deal with that very fear can help them cope with their feelings of angst.

But anxiety is a very treatable disorder, and knowing this has sustained me when I worry about my son, and when I reflect on my own dealings with the ghosts that haunt me. In fact, most children who receive treatment for anxiety show improvement, and among adults, with the right treatment, there can be considerable improvement in their quality of life. I can tackle anxiety at home with a holistic approach that can enable me to enjoy more moments of wonder, joy and calm with Lucian.

It was a few months after I was first diagnosed with anxiety that I sat in the conference room at my son's school on a cold January morning. The room was full to capacity, with some faces that were familiar to me. I had been in this room before, listening to a similar conference about how to manage stress and school work. There is a feeling of familiarity when you go to a place where people make you feel like you are not the only one. And that is exactly the feeling that I needed to feel on that day, a "repeat offender," an out-of-sorts mom who struggles with anxiety.

"Results from the most recent research are staggering. The number one health condition suffered by children in the United States today is anxiety." The opening remarks from Karen Kallis, a respected children's therapist in the community, were pretty concerning. I listened carefully as the speaker explained how children who suffer from anxiety are likely to get their anxiety from their parents. Surely not one parent in that room wanted to recognize that their behavior might be causing anxiety in their children, but as the conference went on it became clear to me that maybe I am one of those parents who, without wanting to, is creating a pattern in the life of their child which is not conducive to peace and calm.

From this school parent conference, I learned that children who suffer from this type of anxiety experience a generalized fear in various areas, such as fear of rejection, even by their parents, and they also experience a lack of security even in their home. Some children are afraid that something will happen to their family, their home, their pet, etc. Between the ages of ten and eleven, generalized anxiety can start showing up in other areas of the life of a child, and it will show more often than not in their performance at school and specifically in academics. By the time the child goes to middle school and high school, anxiety can affect many areas of their life.

"That is exactly what I'd like to avoid," I remember feeling like chanting out loud. What a great idea to have come to this meeting. "I need this! And my ex-husband was right, dang it," I told myself. I took pictures of the slides and I made notes. My head was spinning as I mentally searched for all the times when I had been anxious around my son—too many to count. Surely in the past I've learned that one needs to remain calm around their children and it's common sense that as moms, even when busiest, we should control our emotions, especially in front of our children. I've known this for years. But Karen's message hit a chord somewhere deeper. Beyond staying calm for the sake of keeping "composed" in front of others, there are important reasons I should keep calm in order to provide a better experience for my child. I'm one of the millions of followers of mindfulness talks, and I enjoy yoga and meditation, so I consider myself very aware of how one's energy impacts the rest of the room. But somehow, this time it all seemed to kick me in the butt.

Karen was also suggesting that we as parents begin to teach our children how they should face their fears. What I was learning that morning is that children can live a more productive life by learning how to address their fears with tools of their own. I wanted to better understand how I could prevent my son from suffering from anxiety. I left the conference startled at the revelation that anxiety could permeate the life of children in such a way that it would affect their ability to study, to interact with others, and to have meaningful friendships and relationships at school. I wondered how many of my friends might be suffering from anxiety and how many of them know how to prevent their children from becoming affected by their anxiety in turn.

Beyond congenital factors that can make it more likely for children from anxious parents to suffer from anxiety, parents who suffer from anxiety are more likely to act in ways that can impact the home environment of a child. The message was all the more relevant when it hit me that I was one of these moms.

Later that week, we were at the school playground. My two mom friends, Elizabeth and Juliette, were standing with me as we watched the kiddos play in the manicured fake grass, the slides bright red, the faces lit up with laughter. I was gesturing with excitement as I shared what I'd learned from the conference, which the two moms had missed.

"Of course it's anxiety. I could've told you that, my friend," said Elizabeth.

According to my ever-so-smart close friend, who is also a working mom with an extremely hectic schedule, of course we all have it. Maybe some more than others. But here it is. Here is something that we can be warned about, knowledgeable of, proactive about. We can help guide our children through the ebbs and flows of this early stage in their lives by first taming the dragons inside ourselves. I felt that more than one of my friends might have that dragon fully asleep, if only for a while. I knew I could share the ideas that I've learned through my experience and I wanted to be sure that I mastered the techniques to help manage parental anxiety, some of which I had already begun practicing years ago hoping to bring peace and contentment in my life.

5

Breathe Away the Pain

In the midst of winter, I found there was,
within me, an invincible summer.

— Albert Camus

I admit it. There are times when even scrolling the pages of social media can make me anxious. It's addictive, though. The gazillion messages, birthdays from friends, pictures to see, events that I'm being invited to. The never-ending flow of information and stimulation can at times be too much for my caffeine-enhanced morning brain to handle. Yet I can't get enough. I'm hooked like the rest of the best moms out there.

I know that I'm not the only one who feels this way, yet millions of devoted moms out there seem to successfully juggle their busy lifestyles as working moms. How do some do it? I have no idea. I feel that working moms and stay-at-home moms alike go to tremendous lengths to keep it all together: a home clean, a decent dinner ready, and homework done, as well as making sure their children get to extracurricular activities like sports, music lessons, tutors and medical appointments.

The list goes on and on. The speed at which things happen around me sometimes makes it hard for me to stop and ask the very basic questions that can help assess my current state of mind. Yet asking the right questions can help me as a mom determine the answer to a most important question: How am I doing? And equally important, how is my connection with my child?

I'm not talking about feeling a bit nervous about an upcoming family event. I realize that planning a special dinner or a weekend getaway takes a lot of time and effort. Planning can be supremely time-consuming, not to mention the complexities of coordinating with the various parties involved, including extended family and friends. The type of anxiety that I'm referring to here is not the paralyzing type that some people, unfortunately, experience. The type of anxiety that I refer to is the one that is there all the time and can be triggered easily.

"She calls it healing the heart," said my friend Elisa.

"Who?"

"My therapist. She says healing anxiety is about spiritual matters that need to be cleared."

A compliance official and the mother of a six-year-old girl, my friend Elisa has suffered from anxiety for years. We've been friends for most of our lives. She lived in the same neighborhood where I grew up, in fact a few minutes' walk down the street from my home. We went to the same school, we attended the same college, and we were roommates for two years. Few people in the world know me like my friend Elisa does. Few people can understand where I've been, emotionally and physically speaking. However, when I shared with her the pains of anxiety, she was puzzled.

"Why have we never spoken about this before, Ada?"

Perhaps I have been too busy trying to "survive" it, but the truth is that only until recently did I get clear about my struggles with anxiety. I used to confuse stress with anxiety, until I realized that my obsessive worry was not exactly stress. On the phone with Elisa, I was telling her my story. I shared my anxiety issues with her for the first time.

"I guess I really never felt that I had anxiety until after the divorce, Elisa."

Some people come into your life without any rhyme or reason, while others, like characters in a novel, become pivotal to your own story. As I chat with my old friend, memories of our years together flow softly, gentle and endearing, like a giggle from a toddler inside my head.

"I'd rather have a glass of wine or two than go for meds." She cracks a joke in between, but I know what she is thinking. I know where she is coming from.

"I have my own battles with the meds, Elisa."

"What do you take?"

I love the spirit in which I framed the conversation about antianxiety medication. We moved on to discuss the exact medication that each of us takes, and to my surprise, my friend shared a story about how hard it was getting medication for herself. Finding a doctor that would prescribe it regularly was a challenge, she said. Which got me thinking how lucky I am to have access to wonderful and caring health professionals. Is having access to medication to alleviate symptoms of anxiety such a good thing? We agreed, there are times when you are in a crisis, and at those times, merely breathing in and out will not help. Even a more holistic approach to treating anxiety, like combining meditation with breathing techniques, sometimes is not enough to keep the overthinking patterns under control. Especially during times when anxiety is affecting one's ability to sleep. It is on those days when an anxious mom sees the green light to go straight for the bottle of pills.

"I like to have them, just in case," I said playfully.

As we were getting more comfortable with this unusual topic of our struggles with anxiety, we were reminded of our mundane responsibilities. Chit-chatting about our worries is not a useful endeavor. She had to go to a meeting and I needed to go pick up my son from school. Yet the warm feeling of my friend's kind disposition, her willingness to "go there" with me as I opened up about my issues, her compassion, felt like comforting hands on my shoulders. Her sincere wish was that we could talk again about this very topic.

"Let's talk again, maybe in two weeks?" Elisa said warmly. I could picture her broad smile from thousands of miles away.

These two busy moms knew better than to promise a recurring call that would lead us to commiserate about our struggles in life. We are warriors, we are islanders. We just go with the flow and make things happen, period. As we said our goodbyes, I felt like it hadn't been that long since we last spoke. It's the feeling that you get when you speak to someone who really knows you. It's the assurance from your body that tells you that you are in a familiar place, with a fellow traveler who understands exactly what you are going through. The relief of knowing that you are not being judged because you've kept these thoughts inside for so long.

When I was first diagnosed with depression following my divorce, I didn't dive into the "ifs" and "buts" of my life situation. I was so tired of my daily routine, I didn't care one bit about what type of mental issue I was having—depression, anxiety, who cares? I only knew that I often felt sad and that I couldn't sleep.

"I have never seen a child that has gotten sick as often as yours."

Someone actually said those words to me at work. True story, it happened. Throwing me deeper into a state of anxiety were those less-than-careful people who, not even knowing what I was going through, were not the most sensitive to my challenges. I probably wasn't the easiest person to be around, and I take responsibility for being withdrawn and absentminded. Not just at work, but everywhere. I sometimes felt a complete lack of enthusiasm for anything that was going on around me.

Fortunately for me, there were days when a comment or a compliment from a friend or a coworker would lift me up. Things would ultimately balance themselves out; the people that have a tendency to be caring and compassionate always come through when you need them the most. One day, as the team slowly started to learn about my divorce, I sat down with one of the executives in my division.

"Ada, if you hadn't mentioned it, I would never have suspected that you were going through this."

It was a compliment, words that to this day I remember with a profound sense of gratefulness. His brother was going through a divorce, he knew exactly what it meant for his nephews, and it seemed that it was a difficult time for the whole family.

During those days, friends also came to my rescue with frequent visits, girl get-togethers, and long conversations over business lunches and girls' nights out. We'd pour our hearts out over cocktails and laugh at the most rocky scenes from our lives. My two favorite gals for these sessions were my go-to buddies Miranda and Elizabeth.

Work-related stress aside, I was also having issues with my shoulder. The sharp pain in my left shoulder started to slowly get worse and required me to get a steroid injection. When that didn't work, surgery was my only option. Once again I found myself in the hands of very qualified doctors. The surgeon from St. Joseph's had to go in and shave the bone to get rid of the bone spur. Therapies followed surgery, and all this time I was trying to balance my job and my relationship with my ex-husband. I also was trying to date, which wasn't a very successful endeavor at the time. Healing doesn't come easy, I learned.

The doctor explained that most likely the injury was due to normal "wear and tear"; however, carrying my son up and down stairs and lifting him up from the floor was not helping. The shoulder took a few months to be back to normal. Throughout this time, I could exercise freely for the most part, but I couldn't do much of one of my favorite things: back stretching—more specifically, "downward-facing dog" positions. For many months I wondered if this was how it was going to be for me … after all, I was getting older, right?

Within a year after my surgery, after months of therapy, I slowly got the strength back in my shoulder. I no longer feared hurting myself doing yoga. Before I knew it, I was back to doing the things that I enjoyed the most: swimming, yoga, and also carrying my son to bed.

The wound inside took longer to heal though, much longer. Around this time I had gotten into the habit of finding books that had some kind of substance for me, but also for Lucian. I found a few children's books that talked about mindfulness and affirmation. I thought to myself, "I'm the one that needs to get into this affirmation thing."

I'd get lipstick and write on the mirror of my bathroom: I'm strong, I'm healthy, I'm creative. The words were all the good things that we need to tell ourselves regularly, even when we don't want to believe them, and even when the reality around us is showing us something different.

Every word we choose, every phrase we use to describe ourselves, especially when we are around our children, can shape their view of the world. For example, being over-critical, even when one means well, can affect a child's self-esteem. Instead of encouraging her child, a mom can be causing the child to feel insecure. If the child has the "wanting to please" personality, this could cause him to doubt himself, thus creating a cycle of insecurity and fear at home. The insecurity in turn can make him think less of himself when he is at school, or when he is developing new friendships.

When I read the following advice: "Be impeccable with your words," I couldn't stop telling those around me to think before talking. Think not just one time, but two or three times.

Words can leave a scar in your psyche and those of everyone around you, and especially on the heart of a child.

Creating an environment of love and calmness around Lucian used to be so hard. This anxious mom would go 100 miles an hour; thoughts and to-do lists filled up my mind on a regular basis, and slowing down seemed alien to me. I couldn't afford to slow down because I had too much going on.

The source of most of my stress and worry stemmed from fear, from worrying about my personal situations: balancing work, family and friends. Questioning how my child was doing at school—is he a happy child? How am I doing as a mom? (For a single mom, this one comes often.) I'd go into a never-ending spin mode. I'd wonder if my son's experience in this life was as fruitful as it could be and if I was providing him with the tools that he needed to succeed.

I looked back for traces of trauma in my past that could help shed light on the reasons why I've had these issues, and I found exactly nothing. I had such a positive childhood, a wonderful upbringing in a small city in Puerto Rico, a loving if strict mom and a hardworking if sometimes emotionally unavailable dad. I had two brothers, and older one and a younger one, and a home where we grew up and lived for over 18 years. My two brothers would agree with me that we grew up in a loving home with great support from my mom and my dad. Fast forward to the life that I want to provide for my child, and I wonder, how peaceful is his existence, how calm is his mind? I know that the schedules of divorced homes are a bit more hectic as the child goes from one home to the other. The child often wants to stay in one home and has a hard time returning to the other parent's home. Am I aware of the impact that such an arrangement has on my child?

Children from homes whose parents are together can also be exposed to circumstances that cause a great deal of fear or anxiety in their lives. The father who travels often for work, the mother who stays at home and takes care of the children, often having to also go to work while tending to the house, the dog and an aging parent. Fear that the parent is not coming back might affect some children, especially the young ones who crave the presence of their main caregivers.

Ever since he was a baby, Lucian complained about having nightmares. The inevitable nightly routine was that I would sit in Lucian's bed after reading a book and wait patiently until he could fall asleep. His fear of sleeping alone lasted for years. He would wake up in the middle of the night, grab his favorite blanket, and walk into my room. I would look up and find him standing at the door as if asking for permission to come to my bed. I would oblige, most of the time anyway. The fear of sleeping by himself seemed to get worse as he got older, and I was puzzled.

The nightlight was quite the right amount of light. As Doctor Dennis Rosen's book *Successful Sleep Strategies for Kids* suggests, the level of light has to be bright enough so the child can feel safe, but low enough so that it doesn't interfere with the dozing off of the body. Too much strong light can interfere with the brain's inner clock and delay the body's function as it's trying to fall asleep.

"Can I choose the music, Mom?"

Lucian wants to play DJ and I'm tired and ready to move on to the next step—where he falls asleep—but the soft music seems to be a good way for him to relax and forget about the monsters that might come from under the bed, or the thunder that might strike the roof of our home, or the wolf that might come and eat his pet rabbit, Fluffy.

I keep telling myself that this is only a stage, that it shall pass. But what if it doesn't? What if Lucian's fears when he goes to sleep turn into a larger fear in his life?

Being afraid of things can manifest in a less-than-obvious way. Author Marie Kondo suggests that people who are anxious reflect their attachment to the past or their fear of the future through the things that they own. Her method of decluttering and organizing the home has us facing our fears through evaluating carefully the things that we own. Confidence, she argues, stems from knowing that what we own is what we love. Through learning which things we can do without, our life becomes simplified in more than one way, and thus disposing of things that we don't need will help us have a tidier space and a home that's easier to navigate. I loved the idea that when we teach our children to be tidy and organized, we are also teaching them to be confident in the choices they make.

Although Lucian might be affected by things that I can't control, I want him to be safe from the multitude of questions that affect me every once in a while. I make mental notes of the things that could trigger my anxiety or even Lucian's. In his case, keeping a light on at night is a must.

SURROUNDED BY THINGS

Sometimes I am surprised by the number of products that have made it into our lives; kitchen gadgets help us slice apples more easily, peel fruits and vegetables, make juice and wash lettuce. I'm not advocating discarding tools that can make your life easier, but I find myself longing for fewer things. Fewer things would streamline the process of making decisions on a daily basis.

When my son was a baby, I made the decision that I would only have a limited amount of silverware and baby cups. I wanted to keep only as much as I needed. This way, not only was I making sure that I didn't overspend, but I was using space in my kitchen more efficiently.

I look around my home and sometimes it doesn't reflect the airiness and light that I desire, so I take on the challenge to make my home look like the heaven that it feels like to me. I take a Saturday to put together bags of things that no longer give me a sense of pleasure when I see them in a room. I know that Lucian likes this attitude, although he may not be inclined to give away his toys that easily. I remind him that we want to benefit from a space that is clean and clutter-free. I know that my state of mind will become a reflection of our space.

For me this doesn't come easily, but I've taken it as a continuing challenge in my life. It's normal for toddlers and young children to leave their toys and clothes misplaced, but I know it's a good thing if I can help Lucian take responsibility for his belongings at an early age.

"Please take your uniform off before you sit at the table, Lucian."

I remind Lucian to keep his uniform clean and to put it away after he takes it off at the end of the day. He is still young and most of the time he won't listen or even recognize the value of keeping his clothes clean, but I hope that I can slowly instill the importance of being clean and organized.

"Lucian, it's time to give away some of your toys."

And what happens when I ask Lucian to choose which toys he will give away? Sometimes he is happy to pick toys that he is no longer excited about and he hands them over to me without too much fuss. I place them in a bag, and he seems to be fine. Other times he is reluctant to give away his toys. I must be patient. The little boy has a hard time letting go of his favorite trains, the stuffed animals that he got from his most recent vacation or the birthday present from his favorite aunt.

The room is starting to feel crowded, and I make the effort of helping him choose. I am convinced that the additional effort to minimize the amount of things that surround Lucian will help him in many ways. The more organized things are, the more organized his mind will be and the more room he will have to create.

OUR FRIEND, TECHNOLOGY

If creating a sense of serenity in my life experience is what I'm looking for, I should look no further than my cell phone. Right? I mean, I can find anything I need, from shopping for my favorite clothes to touching base with friends and family via social media.

The habit of checking the social networks has become a problem over the past few years. I want to stay in touch with my friends and loved ones, but I have to control the time that I spend using my phone, especially when I'm with my son.

We should be somewhat concerned about the effects that an increasingly expansive cyberspace has on our lives and on the lives of our children. Researcher Mary Aiken argues that the changes in technology are so abrupt and the impact so broad in countless areas of our lives that human interactions are being changed, and people's state of mind is often being radically changed by "fictional" realities that take over the mind of the user.

From toddlers using tablets to the selfie addiction, cyber relationships and our obsession with a habitual use of social media represents a new form of self-concept is rapidly changing the interactions among adults and youngsters everywhere. But what was most surprising for me to learn as I explored Dr. Aiken's argument is that it's not just children and youngsters who are increasingly affected by the cyber-consumption. Moms too get hooked, and there are clear impacts in the quality of their interactions with their children.

> Joining an online community, or participating in a multiplayer online game, can give you a sense of belonging. Getting your Instagram photos or Facebook posts "liked" meets a need for esteem. But that's just the beginning of social networking rewards and pleasures ... Novelty also triggers these 'feel good chemicals' ... Searching online—whether you are hunting down a piece of information, shop-

> ping for a pair of shoes, or looking for an old
> classmate or professional contact—rewards
> you in another powerful way." – Mary Aiken

I wonder about the impact that using cell phones has on the quality of our interaction with our children. I'm sure it can't be good. While I am not one to download an app that tracks how many times I check emails or go to a social media network, I can be more aware of the times when I grab my phone instead of talking with my son.

"No cell phones at the table, Lucian." I have laid down the rule since he was a toddler. He is growing up in the era of technology, and while I want him to be abreast of the latest, most advantageous technologies, I try to leave the cell phone behind and make room for me and him.

"Let's go for a picnic tomorrow," I announced triumphantly as I ran down the schedule of the day for Lucian. It was April, 2015, and I decided to take Lucian to my favorite place in town more often: a coffee shop by the Chattahoochee River, about ten minutes from our home. I loved it there, but most importantly, I loved the feeling of getting away with my little one even if just for a quick adventure. We would pack our watercolor paint kit, a few blank pages, a few snacks and a couple of waters, along with our blanket and Frisbee, and off we'd go. The sky was always radiant, the greenery fresh after months of specialized treatment that would nourish the soil for the flowers that were to come.

As I walked the long way down the steps, I stopped to look up and take in the perfection of the view. The coffee shop was on my left, built in the '60s, with dark wood and a porch wrapping around the main entrance. On the far right was the pool. The backdrop was gorgeous and the river could be seen from the top of the stairs, the row of trees along the edge giving way to a sitting area for those who sought the sound of the water from up close. Six wooden Adirondack chairs were laid out in a circle waiting for takers. I used to find calm and serenity in days like that. I declared it my PIA, or "Paradise in Atlanta." Around that time, I made it a point to visit my PIA often. The calming waters refreshed me from the inside out. Looking around, I could tell I wasn't the only one who came to this earthly heaven for redemption.

"Let's play Frisbee, Mom!" I oblige, and so the fun begins. Lucian throws the Frisbee and I run around, picking it up from the ground more often than not. His face lights up at the sight of his mom's struggles. This boy has me working *out*, I think. There were times when it was just the two of us, but other times the park would be busy with other children playing nearby.

I guess it might have been easier for Lucian to just play with me the whole time, but because he is an only child I wanted him to start conversations with other children so that he would become comfortable introducing himself and making friends.

I liked the fact that I could encourage him to be more independent while I could watch his interaction with others and make sure that he was safe and comfortable while he did this. Sometimes he'd eagerly walk over to introduce himself, and other times he'd look at me feeling shy. I'd remind him that it was a good idea to make new friends. He slowly started introducing himself more easily, with more confidence.

Looking back, I'm glad that I encouraged him to play with other children. It also gave me a break from running around after the Frisbee. I remember I would lie down on the blanket and I'd watch Lucian starting a conversation. He and a new friend would soon enough be throwing the Frisbee or a football to each other. It was such fun to watch the scene; they looked so happy, so full of life.

"Ducks, Mommy!" And there it is, my favorite part of the outing. We have finished painting and we take a stroll along the river to discover a few ducks who brave the strong touch of the waters of the Chattahoochee. They're in heaven and so am I.

Lucian had turned six and the end of the school year was a few months away. His time in kindergarten would soon end; I almost didn't want it to. The school year was so fun, challenging, adventurous, rewarding, full of moments of laughter. Lucian was still quite the hyperactive little buddy, with lots of energy and a great ability to play sports. It was a special time for little Lucian with birthday parties and school events.

Even I got a chance to participate at a school event as a speaker. With an Earth Day message about the importance of taking care of our planet, I ventured into the classroom of Mrs. Segura to find 14 sunshines waiting to have a fun time. It's all about the arts and crafts, I thought. My son wasn't the quietest one of them, but that would not have surprised anyone. After all, I'm a talkative one myself.

April left and soon came May. The whole family was happy to celebrate with Lucian on his graduation day. Except me, who on that day was having a bit of an anxiety attack. I remember trying to make a decision about Lucian's clothes for that day. Since he didn't like wearing button-down shirts, I felt very stressed out. How on earth am I going to pull this off? A tie? Lucian's sensitivity to certain fabrics had by now taught me to stay away from any attire that would feel funny against his skin.

I couldn't look for options at this point, so I sent a note to the principal: "Can they wear their uniform to the graduation ceremony?"

A day later, the principal sent an email informing all parents that children were allowed to wear the school uniform in lieu of shirt and tie. I was thrilled, I could breathe now. The graduation day arrived, and we were nervous—I should say, I was freaking *out*. Even after being relieved of the stress of getting my son to wear the uncomfortable shirt, I found myself so stressed out and so concerned over everything. What if Lucian hated wearing his uniform? I should've asked him, but I didn't.

And so as we entered the school building, I heard my son complain, "Why is everyone wearing clothes?"

I should have, but I didn't. An hour later his grandparents were asking the exact same question. Arrgh! Luckily, Lucian wasn't the only one in his uniform. I felt anxious for a few hours, yes, but I took deep breaths and just kept going. The day adjourned.

Around this time, I started incorporating other things into my routine, aside from reading and exercising. I now took more time to be outside with Lucian. I made it a point to take him to the park every weekend, and I could see how much he enjoyed the outdoors. In the meantime, I'd sit under a tree with a book in my hand. I would take deep breaths and let go of the concerns, the stuff, that had accumulated throughout the week.

I've chosen a combination of techniques to calm my anxiety. While I've tried many practices individually with good results, I've used a few techniques simultaneously over the years. It's like I'm wearing different hats. These "roles" have become my support system:

DOCTOR TRUTH

- ✪ We try to be all things: the perfect cook, the smartest professional, the best parent, the ideal partner, son or daughter. The truth is that we are all trying our best to be our best. Keeping a journal with a list of the situations that cause anxiety and writing down a statement that challenges the fear created by these situations has helped me.

THE SILENCE MASTER

- ✪ Science has backed the idea that meditating regularly can change our physiology. My favorite time to be in silence is very early in the morning. As soon as I wake up, I turn on my cell phone and play a meditation video, or I spend time just being in silence for about 10 or 15 minutes. When I don't feel like meditating or being in silence, I say a prayer or I listen to soft music. Slow music slows me down, relaxes my brain, makes me feel joyful about things around me, and makes me feel grateful.

THE HEALTH FREAK

✿ Admittedly I'm not a great cook, but I enjoy healthy meals, and when it comes to nutrition I've chosen to challenge anxiety from the perspective of my energy levels. I'm not a dietician, but I know that the darker the colors in your vegetables, the more healthy they are. I've added more vegetables to my diet and I have slowly removed sugar from my diet. Make a special diet for two weeks and see how you feel. I think it's important to share our goals to have a better diet. I've shared my thoughts about consuming less sugar with my son. While he doesn't share the feeling (he loves candy), he is very supportive of his mom's idea to eat less sugary foods.

THE FRIEND

✿ All of us could add to our existing list of friends. It doesn't take a dinner out or a formal invitation; we could start inviting a friend or two to take a regular walk after school or after drop-off in the morning. I remind myself of the benefits of being active, even when I walk to the parking lot. Going for a walk with a friend can also allow us to connect with them. Beyond short interactions at school or at work, when we take the time to go out for a walk, even during lunchtime, we can benefit from having a more meaningful interaction with our friends or our coworkers. I used to go for 15-minute walks around the block with my two coworkers right after lunch, and it made a big difference in my energy level the rest of the day. I not only felt energized but also enjoyed a nice chat with my coworkers.

THE PRESENT PARENT

⚙ Adults spend hours in front of their screens scrolling Facebook, giving "likes" to the world and posting images to let the world know how wonderful their life is. In reality, most people browse their social media pages out of boredom. If you are a parent who spends hours on your cell phone browsing pages without a reason, consider taking a conscious break from technology: "Introducing the seven-day no-technology challenge!" Okay, seven days might seem like a long time to go without checking your phone, but you will find a huge difference in the amount of time that you find on your hands. Take that time to engage in a conversation with your child, plan an activity together, or invite your child to help you with a chore around the house.

When is the last time you heard your child complain about your listening abilities? "You are not listening to me, Mom!"

Even when I think I'm listening to my son, my brain is sometimes too busy trying to organize the next set of things that I have to say so that my son understands what he needs to accomplish to comply with our schedule for the day. I need to be attentive to his needs, and the calmer I am, the more present I will be to listen, really listen, to what he is trying to say. I know that I can be a stronger figure in his life if I can just slow down. Can you relate?

I used to run around with my busy schedule in my head and expect my child to follow through with every event, without making time in the calendar to simply *be* with him. The best part is that it really doesn't take all that much to find moments when I can relax a little and enjoy being with my son. When he was younger, we used to go to a park often and make picnics. I would bring a blanket, a few snacks, coloring books, a Frisbee, and a ball. We'd have the most relaxing time.

Nowadays, we play cards, or I play music and dance around the house and I ask him to join me. Sometimes he just watches as I dance, and other times he requests a special song that he likes, and he joins in the fun. Sometimes, I just sit down and color with my son, and he loves it.

I've learned that children do not need a fancy activity to enjoy being with their mothers. They love the simple expressions of love through words, but even more important, through cuddling and hugging.

TAKING ACTION

There might be a part of you that feels you can help ease tensions in your relationship with your children. Every mother who is dealing with anxiety should decide which practice would work best to address her symptoms. It's like creating a personal plan to succeed in your very personal challenge to control your anxiety.

Breathing in through that fear, getting in touch with that very feeling, is what therapists would have you do to clear that path. There is a blockage inside that causes our hearts to close up, our bodies to get tense, our minds to get overwhelmed. The feeling of being overwhelmed is familiar to those who suffer from anxiety. The good news is that anxiety, regardless of whether it is acute or mild, is a very treatable disorde. If you can recognize symptoms of anxiety in your daily life, there is a chance that your children are feeling a sense of anxiety at home. The tricky thing about anxiety is that, like other mental disorders, it can be difficult to diagnose.

It isn't uncommon for people to confuse stress with anxiety. When we are stressed, we might experience symptoms similar to those we have when we are anxious. However, anxiety and stress are not the same. When we are stressed, it is likely because of a known situation that we are dealing with. However, when we are anxious, we are anticipating things that have not happened yet. When we anticipate a negative outcome to a circumstance, we are feeling anxiety. It is the series of these negative thoughts that can affect our state of mind and also our inner calmness. We become tense, we get headaches, and in some cases, it is harder to breathe.

While meditating by itself can help with some symptoms of anxiety, I've learned that it takes what I call a multi-prong approach to dealing with negative thoughts. Since a tailored approach to things is usually more effective than a "one-size-fits-all" approach, I want to encourage mothers who suffer from anxiety to practice mindfulness techniques and other methods that can help them tame their anxiety. It takes time and it takes practice and discipline to see the results of mindful techniques. It also takes courage to look at yourself and recognize which areas need to be changed.

I'm an advocate of trying various approaches and finding the right approach to dealing with anxiety. I'm also a promoter of establishing a unique plan to deal with one's symptoms. Beyond the ideas that I've listed above—meditation, breathing exercises, and becoming more present in our lives and in our interactions with our children—I believe using a combination of these along with a cognitive therapy approach can make a difference.

Talking to others about their problems might seem like a bad idea to some, who feel ashamed about sharing their most intimate struggles. I've been there. Yet it is through acknowledging the issues that we are having and taking time to analyze the patterns and habits that are making us feel more anxious that we can become the most effective in conquering anxiety.

TAKING THE LEAD

As you plan your approach to dealing with anxiety, I suggest that you look at the things around you, and then start thinking about things you should do internally to create a more calming experience.

CALMNESS AROUND YOU

Below are a few tips regarding environments and living areas that can help promote a more calming space:

⚙ **Declutter your life:** Think about the state of your home. It's almost a reflection of how organized your thoughts are in your brain. I've never considered myself a messy person, but I must admit that keeping a drawer perfectly organized with dividers for socks and underwear can be a challenge. I've found some of the principles of the Marie Kondo's method of organizing a home to be very useful. The idea is that you can simplify your life by having exactly the right amount of things that you need, with things placed in such a way that you can "float" around your home as opposed to feeling oppressed by things in your home. I'm not sure that my home is up to the level of "floating," but you get the picture.

What I've noticed is that when you live in a space that is organized to the point where you can see what you have in each drawer and the clothes are nicely organized in the closet, you are able to appreciate your clothes more. I learned long ago that the morning routine will be easier if I decide what to wear the night before. On weeknights, I pull out the clothes that I will wear (sometimes I allow myself a plan B in case I change my mind), so that the next morning I can save time getting dressed. Similarly, coming home to a clean kitchen gives you a sense of achievement and brings a calming sense to your space. Your children, too, will have a more joyful experience when they have a cleaner space around them.

The benefits of getting rid of things that I don't need as soon as possible are many. I was recently talking with Lucian about ideas to help keep our home more organized. To my surprise, he was excited about the idea of being more organized and clean. I've had him help more frequently with daily chores around the house. I like to compare our chores at home with soccer practice: I remind him that we are a team, and that as such, we have to help each other in keeping our home clean.

○ **Exercise**: The importance of having a regular regimen of exercise can't be underestimated. Most moms spend hours in the car every day, even on weekends. A busy schedule leaves little to zero time for exercise, one of the most basic things for keeping our minds clear and our bodies happy. Going for a walk after dinner with your children, even if only for 15 minutes, can be a good time to catch up with them. You can exercise and at the same time have a few minutes every day for a relaxing conversation with your little one.

○ **The many benefits of yoga**: If you haven't tried yoga yet, please do. Yoga is meant to be a personal practice that benefits the mind and also the spirit. Try to approach yoga as a time to connect with yourself. Through breathing techniques and deep stretching, you can slowly begin to feel that doing yoga is an escape from the daily routine. Another benefit of practicing yoga? When you practice it consistently, you begin to look more carefully at your thoughts. The exercise of paying attention to your thought patterns will, in turn, lead you to ask questions about your emotions. Healing your emotions will lead you to ask questions about your overall experience. Slowly you will begin having more moments of mindfulness, where you are slowing down your thoughts. Expert yogis will tell you that with time, those who practice yoga begin asking themselves deep questions about their life experience, the reasons behind emotions that are causing them angst, clarity about joyful moments, and questions about purposeful living.

○ **Improve your diet**: When I think back to my childhood, I remember with nostalgia how my mother and grandmother would cook delicious homemade meals regularly. Every afternoon after playing outside with our neighbors, we'd head home for dinner. This daily ritual required me to help set the table, wash my hands, and share a prayer before enjoying a meal with my mom and dad. It was the time when we would talk about our day. I try to do the same with my son. I want to cook more and use more organic ingredients in my meals. This is an enduring challenge for moms with a busy schedule, but being aware of the importance of eating more vegetables and fruits, instead of more meat, can be a good start.

○ **Involve children in decision-making:** Letting your children know what's going to happen gives them a sense of control over their schedules. Having a family meeting over dinner on Sunday nights where the family quickly goes over what is going to happen the following week gives children the opportunity to interact, ask questions, give their opinion about things. When we open up the weekly plan for discussion, we are not only letting go of the idea that we are the only ones who have a say about things, but we are also opening up to listening and hopefully asking for help from the rest of the family so that the schedule can run as smoothly as possible.

Setting expectations about schedules and discussing everyone's availability to attend certain events can help everyone in the family feel as if they have been part of the planning of activities. In those times, parents can offer advice to children and give them the chance to voice their opinions, nurturing in them feelings of self-control and empowerment.

When I am busy, I tend to listen less and talk more. I also tend to ignore my own feelings so that I can complete the task at hand. I call this being more emotionally unavailable for my child, and I know that I need to work on this. I often find it difficult to recognize or accept when I mess up or make a mistake. For example, if I forget to pack his soccer uniform, or if I forget to ask his friend's mom if we can get the boys together for a play date, I feel bad admitting it.

Fear, that word again. When I've made a mistake and Lucian points it out to me, I get angry. But the truth is, I fear that admitting to my child that I've made a mistake could make me look weak. If Lucian sees me as a mom who is full of mistakes, I fear he will not listen to my advice in the future. I make up this story and it keeps me from opening up, from admitting, "I messed up, Lucian." Yet, every time I try the difficult approach of opening up about my mistake, I get a surprisingly fantastic reaction from my young son. He is not out to judge me, I realize. My fears lead to a disarming, honest conversation with my eight-year-old.

ELECTRONICS IN OUR LIVES

Not too long ago, I read a post on Facebook about what a woman called the "silent tragedy in America." What this lady was referring to was the lack of parents who are emotionally available for their children. A retired teacher, she suggested that children nowadays are being brought up by computer nannies, and instead of receiving words of encouragement, children grow up thinking they are perfect and special to the point that they don't need to do much to become better. I realize that as moms we feel that our children are special, and they are. But when we tell our children how wonderful and awesome they are, we are not leaving much room for them to want to become better at whatever task it is that they're being tested for.

Anxious parents are less present at times. Believe me, I'm one of them. I struggle with being more present, with slowing down. I'm not judging, because I know from experience how difficult it can be to slow down and listen to our children. However, it doesn't take too much of our time to listen, really listen. And it makes such a difference in the lives of our little ones.

Because I am fully aware of the benefits of slowing down, I have made a conscious effort to spend more time with my child doing simple things, like reading a book, throwing a ball for a few minutes, or eating dinner side by side.

How many families do you know who sit at the table for breakfast and dinner every night? A friend shared with me the situation at their home where her teenage daughter, like many her age, felt a total disconnect with her mom. Though she was a devoted mom, she worked every day, and by the time she got home she felt exhausted and oftentimes removed from her daughter's most personal and intimate feelings. Her daughter would sit in front of the TV to have dinner, leaving her mom at the table eating alone. Does this scenario sound familiar? For me, TV is no longer the main concern nowadays. Access to tablets is.

"Can I have the Kindle now, Mom?"

It's been a few years now since the last time I let Lucian use my iPad. He broke the first iPad I ever had, a highly desired item back in the day, a present from my boss which I was so excited to get. Lucian dropped it on the garage floor and its screen smashed in tiny pieces. Soon enough it went dark. Lucian is older now, and like every child that I know, he hasn't outgrown his love affair with technology. Like millions of children his age, he will spend countless hours playing with his tablet, even watching TV at the same time if I don't control it.

Connecting with your children requires that you are willing to open up and be honest about your most personal feelings. You can't preach something that you don't practice, and as you know children will only learn by seeing you act in the way that they should emulate. Teaching by example can't be underestimated. Maybe you can start changing the way you've felt about sharing your insecurities with your children.

There is a well-known study done in the 1960s by Dr. Walter Mischel, called *The Marshmallow Test*, which is familiar to most primary school teachers. The study exposed the importance of teaching children about regulating their impulses. It showed that children *can* wait before eating their favorite candy and that teaching your children to control their impulses and emotions will without a doubt be of great benefit to them in life. But how do you go about it when you as a parent have a hard time controlling your own impulses—overeating, using your cell phone all the time, talking on the phone while driving, or watching TV until you fall asleep. These are all bad habits that as parents we try to ditch on a regular basis.

Recently I found myself telling Lucian the story of my two big teeth. Anyone who knows me from childhood will tell you that I had the biggest front teeth that they had ever seen. For three or four years before I got braces, I was miserable at school. Some of the boys would make fun of me, and even my brothers would call me names when we got into arguments.

As I told the story to Lucian, I had a clear intention of letting him know that I was a child once. I know how it feels to wear eyeglasses and be made fun of because of the way I looked. I told Lucian that there are things we can't control, but I know he knows this already. I became very good at concealing these two teeth, and in every picture I would hide them. Looking back, it may be the same way I conceal other fears and insecurities at this stage in my life.

Every time there is a misunderstanding with my son, instead of blaming him I ask myself the question, "What happened?" I explore the responses that I come up with and try to understand my role in the situation. More often than not, I can identify ways in which, with a better approach, I could make things easier on my son. Instead of jolting out with a quick response, a demand, or even a firm request, I try to go to a place where I can have a conversation.

LOOKING ON THE INSIDE

Now that we've covered the external factors that could be addressed to improve our environment and make our spaces more calm, we can begin working on the inside of ourselves. This next step is the most important in healing our anxiety.

This requires me to listen, and listening requires that my mind is clear and receptive to the ideas that my son is going to share. Below are a few tips to help you start creating a space of calm:

- ⚙ **Breathe in and breathe out**: In order to calm down the voices that rise up in our minds, buddhists and cognitive therapists suggest breathing exercises to clear the mind and to help us focus our attention internally. When you breathe deeply, you can focus on how the air is coming in and out of your body. Deep slow breaths can help us relax, especially if we close our eyes while taking slow deep breaths. Breathing exercises allow the mind, which is identifying with the thoughts causing fear, to slowly start to focus on the passing of air through the mouth and into the lungs.

⚙ **Meditate:** Have you tried meditation yet? The benefits of meditation are now well documented by science. There are numerous free videos and apps that you can download to your cell phone and access anytime. I've found myself meditating in the morning or early in the evening, but sometimes even in the afternoon I might retreat to meditate and recharge. Not only can meditation help us find calmness inside when we need to take a break from the stress of the day, but also our children can benefit from learning how to sit still and breathe deeply to calm themselves down.

⚙ **Embrace silence**: We've gotten so used to the noises in our lives. The radio plays a never-ending trail of songs, and our houses are filled with the noise of TV. If you are like me, in addition to the outside noises, your mind is filled with constant ideas and thoughts that show up unannounced. Find time to just sit quietly and empty your mind of all the noise and all your thoughts. If meditating is not working for you, perhaps start by spending a few minutes in silence every morning before getting out of bed. Try to think about nothing, and focus only on your breath. This practice can help you start your day with a clear mind, a sense of gratitude, and a relaxed sensation in your body.

- **Explore nature:** If heading out for a weekend getaway to the beach or the mountains is not an option, visiting nearby parks can offer moments to experience nature. Going to a park that has tall trees and water fountains can help us tune out the noise from our minds. Nature reminds us of the perfection of the creation, and it can help us get back to a place of calm within. Visiting a nature trail or a park with our children provides a much-deserved relaxing time away from traffic, emails, or even long phone conversations that can be exhausting. When you visit nature, try to place your attention on the trees, or try to listen attentively to the birds singing. Encourage your children to find a beautiful flower, or ask them what is their favorite tree or their favorite game to play at the park.

- **Talk to your closest friends**: In previous chapters I've mentioned how having great friends has helped me heal my anxiety. Their friendship, and especially their willingness to listen, has helped me process things over the past few years. Whenever I've experienced hurt, pain or heartbreak, my friends have helped me get unstuck. They have not only patiently listened, but also they've offered a different perspective on a situation. Looking at things from a different perspective has helped me move from a place where I find myself stuck.

- **Write to release your emotions:** Writing has been therapeutic for me in so many ways. I feel like the practice of putting my thoughts and feelings in words helps me organize them, and there is a process of validating what I'm feeling, which helps me release my emotions as I write them down.

☉ **Engage your creative side:** Writer Elizabeth Gilbert talks about the beautiful creative force within each one of us and how it's been there all along, waiting to be set free. Whether you feel that you are a creative person or not, there is something that is a source of joy in your life. Maybe you like to read, and when you read you feel as if you've left your body for a minute and are reaching the clouds. Or perhaps you like to color, or paint. You once attended a workshop with oil-painting lessons and discovered that you weren't as bad at painting as you thought. Maybe you enjoy singing on Sundays when you go to church. You don't have to have the voice of an angel to notice if singing in the shower makes you especially relaxed. When you tap into your creative side, you release a creative energy that yearns to be set free. However unsophisticated, try doing that thing that brings you joy more often and you will start discovering a source of bliss within.

Creating calmness in my child starts with me: being more present, consciously making a point to keep emotions in check, and regularly finding a way to get centered before having conversations with my son. As the years go by, I find that it's easier to master this venture.

I've realized that an additional benefit to getting closer to my child is enjoying a deeper connection with him. I feel that I understand him better. I am in control of my anxiety and feel that I have a good idea of how Lucian is feeling on a daily basis. It gets easier with time because I've made a habit of using the techniques shared above. It has yielded to more times when Lucian and I can get closer and connect in a deeper way.

Section II

How I Created a Deeper Connection with My Child

6

Build a Bridge

Be the king of your kingdom.

— Wayne Dyer

Have you ever been in a situation where your child has acted defiantly, as if deciding that he is not going to listen to you?

I've had moments with Lucian when I've felt that he was not listening to me, not following my instructions. I wondered if it was something that I was doing wrong or if he simply was an unruly child.

Back when Lucian was in kindergarten, the teachers pointed out one time that, after being given specific instructions to stay inside the playground, Lucian turned around and a few minutes later was opening the gate to go outside and pick up his ball, which had flown out over the fence and into the parking lot.

I wondered if my five-year-old was starting to become unruly and defiant against the teacher's authority. I worried that his behavior could not only put him in a dangerous situation at school but that it was an indication of his future temperament.

"Am I raising a child that is disrespectful?"

I couldn't help but wonder if there was something I was doing wrong at home that might cause my son to act up at school. Maybe he was being defiant, or maybe he wanted to call attention to himself in a bad way. I was in close contact with the teachers, and I always showed an open heart to any of their suggestions. Instead of reacting, or responding in a defensive manner, I was open to the possibility of listening to the advice of those who have been trained to teach. After all, being a first-time mom, I could learn a thing or two about raising a preschooler.

Looking back, I was smart to have this attitude about things. I learned about many aspects of my son's personality and temperament, beyond his being hyperactive by nature, that helped me look at him in a more compassionate way. I'd sit down and ask Lucian, "What happened?" And I'd sit patiently and listen to what he had to say. I didn't assume that he was wrong, and I didn't assume that he intentionally wanted to break the rules at school. I would then explain to him the consequences of his behavior. His safety was at risk.

I would remind myself that I should put into action these basic principles:

a. Reinforce good behavior.
b. Use simple language that allows Lucian to follow exactly what I want to convey.
c. Focus on my son's good behavior instead of his bad behavior.

   d. Lift his self-esteem through careful praise instead of constant recognition that is not sincere.

When I'm in an anxious mode, however, it can be extremely hard to have a conversation about a moment like this, when my child has clearly broken the rules, and when he needs my guidance. It is in those moments when I need to watch very carefully the words that I say and also the message that I'm sending through nonverbal communication.

PRESCHOOL YEARS

"Preschool years are a time of learning for
a child and their parents, especially for first
time parents."
— Sal Severe

Dr. Sal Severe, a respected authority in the field of parenting and psychology, argues that children's behavior is a result of their temperament and our parenting style. It might seem like an obvious conclusion to anyone who has been a parent for a while, but I was completely overwhelmed by the amount of information that I was receiving from all angles when Lucian entered preschool and throughout kindergarten. His developmental milestones were met, but there were hyperactive issues, there were attention issues, and I realize now that I was looking at myself in the mirror—I was just like him when I was growing up. Not only that, but perhaps some of the behavior-related issues had to do with me? Perhaps I was discovering behaviors in him that were a result of my style of parenting? Perhaps those areas could be addressed and easily changed? Unfortunately, I didn't have many of the tools that I have now, and there are a million things I know now that I simply didn't know then.

I am able to model behavior and I'm able to be more understanding of the different stages in the development of a child. I realize many of my challenges had to do with my child's own personality and genetics, but I would be unfair to blame everything on that and not take responsibility for the things that I could've done differently during the preschool years. I know that I was engaging in behavior that needed to change in order for me to have better communication with my son.

We often hear the old "monkey see, monkey do" advice from elders, and I found myself watching my every behavior to make sure that I wasn't being a bad role model for my son. Modeling behavior for Lucian didn't come naturally for this anxious mom. Don't get me wrong, I don't consider myself the disrespectful type, quite the contrary. However, around the time when Lucian was four and five, I remember feeling so extremely overwhelmed by the increasing demands of being a single parent and a working mom that I had very little energy to focus on modeling behavior for my child.

The adage rang true then as it does now. I struggled with the very basic principle of effective communication: actively listening to my son. Each day, on my way to pick him up at the after-school program, I would be so excited to see him. Just seeing his sweet little face was the moment I was waiting for. Such a small thing, right? Yet my inability to focus on the task at hand would often get in the way. I would find myself hopping on the phone as soon as I got in the car, the conversations often with my boss, and this was not conducive to my having a relaxed state of mind before picking up Lucian. It wasn't because the conversations were stressful, it was the active mind going around and around, analyzing, strategizing, and planning for the next day of activities at work, until I would become distracted and absentminded. By the time I arrived to pick up my darling child whom I had been missing all day long, I'd be in a trance. I was there but *not really* there.

I'm not implying here that it is wrong to have a phone conversation when we are on our way to pick up our children from school, but I think it would be helpful to be mindful of how this behavior affects children. If I want Lucian to listen to me, then I need to learn how to listen to him. And listening is not possible if I have my cell phone in one hand and my bag in the other.

By the end of the day, the little boy was ready to see me, too. Except that by the time that I picked him up, it was closer to 6:00 p.m. Aside from my tiredness from work, I would find my child in an equally exhausted mode.

"Mommy, I'm hungry."

The snacks at the after-school program were delicious. However, I think what Lucian meant to say was "I'm hungry for your attention, Mom." It happened more than once. His hunger would then turn into a long whining session. Because we live about 30 minutes from school, this whining would often turn into crying. Before I knew it, I had a crying preschooler in the back seat demanding food, his bed, his blanket, a movie, or dessert. The list would go on and on, and upon listening to my preschooler's load of demands, I would often shut down emotionally. My internal dialogue would be something like this: "Are you kidding me? I've been working all day long to come to this?"

The excitement and anticipation of seeing my son after a hard day at work would soon turn into a regretful moment. I'd feel angry at him because I couldn't understand why he would be so tired, so hungry, so whining, so needy. With time, I slowly understood that what my son craved was time with his mom. Lucian craved my attention, my listening ears, my hugs and my kisses. Simply that.

Around this time I learned about the importance of understanding my child's love language. I had thought that my words of encouragement when Lucian was feeling down would help him, but I soon learned that Lucian preferred expressions of love in the form of hugs and kisses. How did I learn this? By asking him. Learning my son's love language showed me how to connect with him in a way that made him feel fully loved and fully understood. The wonderful thing about children in the preschool years is that they are so pure and so naïve. What they tell you comes from such an honest and innocent place. Sharing those beautiful exchanges with my son brought me such joy. It also made me feel that as a mom I was on my way to developing a very special bond with my son.

Who doesn't want a very special bond with their children?

Crickets. I thought so. And it took me a lot of effort to understand that I needed to take a step back, to take more time to be with my son, to listen patiently, and to be more present for him. All the while, I was dealing with my own anxiety and stress issues that come with balancing your work with your personal life. My mom never worked full-time, and I think the three of us kids greatly benefited from having her present all the time. Not only was she present in body, but she was also present in heart and soul—in spite of the countless times when my brothers and I literally brought down the house with our fights and screaming matches, in spite of her having to run after us with a broom. (That time was hilarious. I can't recall the details but I can remember that she was very mad.)

In order for us to have a very close bond with our children, we need to provide an environment for a relationship to be built. Instead of coming to the interaction with my son with an attitude of "I'm your Mom and you will do this because I said so," I began to choose a more compassionate approach to my interactions with him. I've already shared how I used to spank Lucian when he was a toddler, and I feel that it was not the best approach to parenting, but at least I passed that stage and was able to slowly learn to instill a different rhythm around him.

There are a few things that are positive about being divorced and raising a young child as a single parent that I think are worth sharing: when I come home with Lucian, regardless of how mad at him I've been, or how mad with me he was, I have the guarantee of a completely controllable environment in my home. And by controlled environment, I mean silence and peace.

You might wonder why I'm so focused on the stories that have to do with the way our mind works and its effects on our emotions. I've been obsessed with the subject of mindfulness for years, and it all stemmed from the realization that I'm often negotiating with my own mind about which thoughts I allow to come in. I had lived the better part of my early life not being aware of the power that negative thinking can have in our daily lives, and in my early twenties I was invited to a conference in Atlanta. It was a "New Age" type of affair, and among the speakers was a man who had already impacted the life of millions through his messages of mindfulness: Dr. Wayne Dyer. It was the early 2000s and I had been working two or three years at Turner when I had the opportunity to sit at Wayne's talk. After he was finished with the presentation, I walked up to him and exchanged a few words. To this day, I remember the compassion in his words and in his demeanor. He was one of those people that make you feel more at peace just by being around them. From Wayne I learned to be aware of the thoughts that I let inside my mind.

From Eckhart Tolle, also a famed author on the subject of mindfulness, I learned the power of being present to my current circumstances, regardless of how difficult my life experience is. If I can choose the way that I look at things, things might start looking different for me.

Aware of my mindless patterns, I decided a few years ago, before I had Lucian, that I had to be aware of the things that were affecting my perception of things around me. It has taken years to master the technique of catching myself when my mind is going to a place of sadness, of anger, of guilt. I enter into a dialogue with myself, and I ask, "Is it true?"

Coming back to the subject of building a bridge with our children, I've understood from my years as a marketing communication professional that I need to be in the right set of mind to enter into fruitful communication. This not only applies to my child, but to everyone around me. I'm responsible for setting my mindset so that I'm able to talk and listen to my child. I'm pretty sure that many mothers will agree with me that it would be helpful to learn what the patterns of our thoughts are so as to understand the pitfalls and the tricks that our minds set for us.

The one thing that has pointed the way for me to build a strong bridge to communicate with my son is to stop and listen to what's going on inside. Stopping and listening to my thoughts, and stopping and listening to the conclusions that I might be arriving at. Those very conclusions should be something that I listen to more often for the purpose of self-exploration. However, I can't overthink when I'm with my son, because if I do that then I miss the moment with him. And the reality is that he feels it.

Lucian can tell when I'm there with him but not *really* there with him. Sometimes it's so terrible, this way of overthinking, that even as I listen to Lucian when he is telling me a story, before he finishes I might already be arriving at a conclusion in my head: "Where is he going with this? Is he going to tell me that he got in trouble at school, or is he going to tell me that he's hungry?" I think smart mothers tend to overthink and overanalyze, and in doing so we get in the way of our children's ability to express themselves freely when they are around us.

THINKING MORE THAN BEING: TIPS FOR MINDFUL PARENTS

I want to pay attention to what I'm thinking and to the things that I'm assuming at times, which might not be based in reality but might be a result of my persistent patterns of overthinking. In my case, overthinking as a mom is easily manifested in how tight I want to have a handle on things around me.

Why do I need to feel that I have to control my son's actions or the actions of others around me, if not because I'm afraid? I face the question of fear in my life—again. I realize that I will have to face this question on a regular basis, and I've learned to make peace with it, as I mentioned before. But if I want to establish a more peaceful environment so that I can be more present for my child, and so that I can listen more attentively to him, I must learn what "being" looks like for me. Let me explain where I'm going with this.

If "being" for me means having a job that pays the bills, having a child that fares okay at school when he could be doing better, having a home to sleep in and a couch where I can watch TV comfortably with a bowl of ice cream in my hands, then there is a certain level of "thinking" that will be required. If, however, I want to set my expectations of "being" a bit higher, saying for example that I want to *enjoy* every day in my job, or that I want to *cherish* the moments I get to spend with my son, or that I want to *thrive* spiritually speaking, every day, then I have to hold myself accountable to a higher standard. Getting there will require that I go deeper into my areas of gray and start allowing some light inside.

Spanking aside, there is something to be said for the strict parenting that some of us had back in the day. When I grew up, you didn't raise your voice to your father because the consequences were severe, and parents didn't look to be friends to their children. I know I never considered my mom to be my friend, and looking back I think she had the right approach to parenting. Not perfect, but right. Everyone can choose the style of parenting that works best for them, and it is not my intention to judge or tell anyone how to parent. However, I've learned a few principles along the way that have served me well:

- **Reminding our children that we love them:** Regardless of the situation, I knew that I could count on my mom's unconditional love. I was a handful and she had two other children to care for, but I never questioned how much my mother loved me. Even when she was the harshest in her punishments over things that might not have been that big of a deal. She would always come back to a place where we could talk about what had happened, and I would feel supported at home. I felt that home was a safe place. There were very few arguments between my parents, and I can remember how sad I felt to see them argue. Yet I remember that both of them, especially my mom, would make the effort to shield us from any argument that she and my dad were having.

- **Building the foundation of a good relationship with our children:** Trust is the key foundation to my relationship with Lucian. In order to build a bridge of communication with my son, I knew I had to create serenity around him, allow him to express himself freely, and even when he wouldn't comply with my every requirement, let him feel that he could do things on his own. This building of trust between us has grown since those early years that I felt were challenging for me in many ways. I have found sources of advice in my family, friends, teachers, parenting tools that are available for free, and even the public library. I've gained insights on modeling behavior for my son, even when I'm not excited about showing him what I'm trying to show him; for example, how to be respectful to others.

● **Showing our children the importance of giving to our community:** In Arecibo, where I grew up, my mom would often volunteer at church. When I say volunteer at church, I don't mean dropping a few dollars in the offering plate, shaking hands with guests, and helping distribute flyers at the door. My mom was a catechism teacher, she would volunteer to be part of the chorus, and she was a reader during the service. To my embarrassment at the time, my mom was at church often. Now, I'm not suggesting that all parents become as active in their church as my mom was, but what I'm trying to illustrate is that children learn humility and respect by seeing their parents behave in a way that shows how humble and respectful they are toward religious figures, or teachers when they are around.

⊛ **Being humble and showing our children how that looks:** Beyond respecting elders and teachers at my school, I grew up looking at the religious leaders in my community with a lot of respect. They set an important example for us and we had a healthy dose of fear growing up among nuns and teachers. We were careful not to get in trouble. As I look back I find so much value in the principles that religious and community leaders instilled in my life as I grew up. The local Girl Scout leaders and volunteers at local groups in our community—I didn't appreciated them much when I was a child, yet their presence in my life throughout my formative years was important. I credit my mom and dad for instilling a sense of deep appreciation for the service of those who gave of their time willingly and without expecting any compensation. In terms of respecting religious leaders, watching my mom pray taught me about the importance of going to church, looking at others around you and smiling with a sincere desire to be there, to participate and be part of the community. Parents teach through their actions, not through their words.

A visit to the Catholic parish near my home about a year ago made me wonder about the importance of kneeling down at church. I was sitting behind a family of four, a father, mother, and two young adults. They were visitors to the parish, or so it seemed. Right in the middle of the service, when everyone was kneeling down, I watched as the father sternly told his son not to kneel. I found it odd and was a bit offended. As much as I respect his beliefs, even if only a visitor, I felt that out of respect for those around him, he should kneel down, or at least bow his head as a sign of respect. I felt then that his attitude was wrong; just like when you visit a home where you have been invited, you follow the lead of your host.

I learned from watching how my mother behaved around others; she showed me the importance of the values of service, compassion, humility, and respect for authority. I am convinced that seeing my mom doing charity work, offering her time to teach children from the most impoverished communities in Arecibo, and offering to help without expecting anything in return, has instilled in me the desire to do the same for Lucian.

In Atlanta, I volunteer regularly during the religious services that I attend, and sometimes I bring Lucian with me. Often he complains, "Mommy, I don't want to go to church!" I can relate, because I used to complain when my mom would take me to volunteer at an event. However boring it might seem to him, I continue to take him, and I tell him: "I know it's not fun, but life is not all fun and games. They need my help, so I help." I always try to volunteer, and not just at church, but at community events or for nonprofit organizations. It doesn't matter where I volunteer, as long as I'm working for the greater good.

One day Lucian will be old enough to make his own decisions. He will get to decide if going to church is for him. Maybe, like me, he will grow up and choose not to go so often, but he'll pick up a project and volunteer from time to time. Maybe in the future, as he gets a few grays in his beautiful head of hair, he will agree that kneeling down in silence to connect with the Lord in the presence of a community is not such a terrible idea.

BEING PLAYFUL

Looking for moments when I can connect with my little one has made me more playful. I've noticed that even when I have to talk about something that I know Lucian will not be thrilled about, like, for example, signing birthday cards or daily chores like making his bed, I can anticipate what he will like to get as reward and act playfully about it. I have to admit that at times I've replaced time out and spanking with bribing. That's right. I'm sorry to admit that I do bribe my son to agree to do little tasks like these, and it works like a charm. I try to leave it up to him, and I remind him that it will be his choice: "If you don't make your bed you won't have dessert tonight."

I've picked up on ideas from Lucian's teachers at school about the ways that I can strengthen my connection with him. Complimenting one another is something that I need to teach. Lucian, I've learned, is very open to complimenting not only me but also his friends and family, because he was taught how to do this at school. Instead of telling a child that he is good or bad, I learned that we should refer to his decisions as right or wrong choices. Schools nowadays have such innovative ways to teach wonderful values to our children, and when I pay attention I can quickly learn to reinforce what my son learns at school.

I've improved my ability to connect with my son by speaking in the same language and at the same level as he is. Because I'm not a teacher, there is a lot that I've had to learn over the years, concepts that I never was taught when I was a child. For example, Lucian came home one day talking about "how to fill someone else's bucket." As he shared the details, I slowly picked up on the concept that we all carry an invisible bucket that can be filled with words of encouragement. The popular children's book called *Have You Filled a Bucket Today?* quickly became my favorite. The idea is that you go through your day either "dipping into the bucket" or "adding to the bucket" with kind words and gestures. I gladly took to heart the ideas shared in this book. Since I heard about this book I began to talk in terms of the choices that Lucian has made instead of making it personal. For example, instead of telling Lucian that I am disappointed on him because of something he did, I would point out that he made a poor decision and therefore I felt disappointed. I reinforce the fact that he is able to make better choices next time.

When we start to see more clearly these futile, relentless patterns at work, we can feel a mix of disenchantment, a yearning for more meaningful pursuits, and a sense of compassion for the poignancy of the human condition. That can be a motivator to wake up, in the ways we've been asleep.

— *Mind Whispering*, Tara Bennett-Goleman

Making better choices and knowing how to be pleasant wherever you go applies to Lucian's anxious mom as well. I've chosen to be a pleasant mom even when I'm stressed or worried or tired. Though being a single parent has afforded little free time, I have learned to appreciate the silence that I've created around Lucian, especially at home when there is silence and I can share moments of peace and calm. We play cards, we play chess, we listen to music and dance around the kitchen. I know that my son feels safe when I can provide more of those moments at home when there are no arguments, no bickering, just calmness and joy. Being present and pleasant takes me a long way with my son. I've noticed that when I check myself and get myself "back in line," I can be more effective as a communicator.

Listening without trying to anticipate what he has to say has taught me that I can let go of the need to control every single situation. Smart working moms, we suffer a great deal from this. Even when we don't realize it, we want to control, and the more we control the less strong is the foundation of our communication with our children.

7

Teaching through Example

Children and adolescents are more likely to listen to adults they perceive as fair, empathic, and respectful than to adults who seem arbitrary, inconsistent, and angry.

— *Raising Resilient Children*, by Robert
Brooks and Sam Goldstein

I often wonder what career path my son will take when he grows up. Will he be a doctor who helps those who are sick and brings hope to those who need it the most? Will he be an engineer, figuring out how to resolve the most complex problems in construction, or will he be a science researcher trying to find treatment for the strangest of viruses? Will he be a soccer player, as he likes to say, or maybe an "ice cream seller," as he recently announced he'd be? Whatever career he chooses, I tell him I will support him.

There was a time when I wanted to be a psychologist. The idea seemed logical to me. I was a people person and I liked to help others. I also enjoyed offering ideas and trying to tell people what they should do. As a dominant personality, I was sure that I could be a good psychologist. That is, until I sat down with the school's student counselor. It was 1990 and I was in my junior year. I was already planning my exit from high school and my way out of Arecibo, the hometown that I grew to love but a place that couldn't offer the experiences that I was looking to have in my future as a college student.

Mrs. Eloise had black short hair, round eyes, and a gentle voice. She was more than a counselor at our school. She was pleasant, yet serious and professional. As I sat across her desk, she carefully looked at the results of the career aptitude test that I had taken a few weeks before, as I made my case as to why I should apply for a career in psychology. I remember being puzzled by the conversation and I left the meeting feeling very confused.

"Communications." Mrs. Eloise's suggestion that I explore a different career choice seemed odd to me.

Since I was a girl, I had liked reading and enjoyed writing even more. I was an extrovert and I wasn't exactly one to sit around all day. She simply couldn't picture this ball of fire listening patiently to eight or ten people a day as they dumped their load of situations on me.

So I changed my mind about my career path and decided to choose a degree in communications. I was accepted to the prestigious University of Puerto Rico, Río Piedras Campus. Their mass communications program was highly regarded, and I was very excited to join a few other friends from school who also were attending college there.

My four years were pretty much a blast, and looking back I realize I was very lucky to have had the expert advice of a person like Mrs. Eloise. Not too long ago, I decided to reach out to this wonderful counselor who had saved me from enrolling in a career that was possibly far from a good option for me, given my personality, and especially after finding the career of communications a true fit. I sent her a message via Facebook messenger: "Dear Eloise, (I decided at this point in my life I could drop the formality) "I always remember how you persuaded me and convinced me to go for a career in mass communication. I truly appreciate your advice."

This, coming from a student whom she saw graduate from high school over twenty years ago. She replied candidly, letting me know she was happy to see that I had found the right path.

I hope that I can be like Mrs. Eloise for Lucian, but if I want Lucian to listen to my advice, I had better stay calm and collected throughout the next ten years of his life. Ten years! Wow, they seem like a lot, but I know they'll go by quickly.

I try to be the counselor for my son when I can. There might be, after all, a hidden teacher in me who wants to share as much advice as I can in the few years that I'll have my son living with me. I know he will be a better communicator if I teach him how to communicate in an effective way. For example, I'm very open about sharing things that are making me anxious:

"Son, please just do what I ask you to. Don't do anything that could distract me, I need to stay focused."

"You know I get very nervous when I travel. I want to be sure that I don't forget anything."

Remembering things can be another source of stress. I have to drive my son to school and make sure that he has everything ready—schoolwork done, papers signed, soccer gear ready, allergy medication taken, etc. The list of things that a mom has to remember every morning goes on and on. I try to anticipate things as much as I can without being too rigid about what's coming our way.

Weekend activities are planned in advance. I talk to Lucian about weekend activities so that we can think ahead about what's needed. I ask Lucian what he would prefer in terms of weekends because I realize that during the week there is so much to do and so few chances for him to choose. I try to allow him to choose when possible, as I think it is important for our children. Having them feel free to express what they feel about their future is important, too. In trying to create more spaces of calmness, I want to have more opportunities for conversations with my child where I can listen to him, *really* listen to him.

Understanding anxiety and how it manifests in our lives can help us recognize moments when we can promote more calmness around our children. In the chapters ahead, I'll address specific techniques to help you deal with anxiety and maintain an atmosphere that is free of stress, judgment, or tension around your children.

Just like when you are dealing with your own anxiety, delving deep inside to discover the areas that might be affecting you, there will come a point when you will want to sit down and reflect on your child's reactions to moments of anxiety.

What works for me has also proven to help ease my son

during times of stress. I apply the steps of revealing, meditating, health freak, and teacher to my child. The idea is that when I think about my son in the presence of situations that cause him anxiety, I can address things at the right level.

As with other matters that pertain to motherhood, I try to have a sense of humor. It is precisely because I can often be serious and overly stressed with Lucian that I try to take on a different role when I'm working through my anxieties.

THE EXPLORER

○ Let's see which things are bothering my son. Is he more anxious when he goes to bed at night, or when he goes to school in the morning? I ask questions that can help reveal my child's state of mind. I like to inquire about the day and try to get him to let me know what the best part of his day was. I ask him, "Why?" to really learn more about him and his likes.

Instead of assuming what the experience of a child is, we can try to encourage him or her to tell us what they are thinking. We can encourage them to look around and discover things by themselves. Let them come up with stories, ideas, or imaginary friends. All of the above are fine by me as long as he is exploring new territories, making new friends, and engaging in new environments. It doesn't have to be a fancy vacation every time, all it takes is the spirit of exploring. "Let's go for an adventure," I'd sometimes announce to my son with a broad smile on my face, showing excitement about our next exploit. It wouldn't be a long drive or even a long walk. Normally, I'd invite Lucian to go for a walk around the block. I'd ask that he bring his soccer ball with him, and we'd go to a green area nearby and kick the ball for a while. I'm always surprised at how little this child needs to feel like he's had a lot; what seems like a few minutes to me feels like a whole afternoon full of excitement to him.

THE TAPPING MASTER

✪ By now you can imagine that I'd be open to trying new ways to help my anxiety. I have found myself tapping my forehead, my chin, my collarbones and the top of my head. It's not like I lost my mind, but I decided to look for new options. I'm also curious and willing to learn new things so I decided to try tapping, or EFT (Emotional Freedom Techniques). I had heard of it, but decided to try it only recently and I was surprised with the great results. It is considered a "modern" technique for dealing with anxiety. Tapping originates in Chinese medicine and its method aims at interrupting the energy patterns that cause emotions that stem from pain and anxiety, among others. Think acupuncture, but without the needles. The idea behind this therapy is that there are areas of your body where nerve endings can be massaged to alleviate the tension that is building up in your muscles and, some argue, traveling throughout your whole body. When you massage certain points in your body— above your eyebrows, under your eyes, at the collarbone or on top of your head, for example—you are sending a message directly to the amygdala area in the brain. This part of the brain has been shown in research to perform an important role in the way we process fear and other emotional responses.

Adding tapping to the equation only came about recently, and I've felt the difference that tapping has made for me. I thought I'd share my experience with tapping for those who might be curious about what EFT involves and might want to try it. There are specialists who provide EFT therapy, and there are plenty of free online videos that provide phenomenal guidance for those who want to try tapping at home.

I was skeptical at first, but the idea that touching yourself in the forehead can distract you from your obsessive thinking is genius. The first time I tried tapping, I admit it: it felt funny. I was sitting in my bed watching a YouTube video that talked about the benefit of tapping to help with various symptoms of anxiety, and I didn't feel anything special.

A year later, I tried it again, this time with my therapist. I'm not sure that anything special happened then either, but I felt like I was "getting the hang of it." The third time I tapped, I really felt different. I remember it clearly. I was in the middle of traffic and I felt a rush of blood coming to my head. I decided maybe it was a good time to distract my brain, and tapping seemed like a good idea. I'm not sure if experts of EFT would agree with me, but at that point I was a bit desperate.

The logic behind tapping makes the most perfect sense to me: by interrupting the thought patterns of your brain you can release feelings of negativity. It's described as a treatment that reaches points in your nervous system in different parts of your body that channel energy to your brain, like acupuncture but with your fingers. And so, in that moment when I was in the middle of traffic, sitting in my car, I started tapping. I felt it!

There was a slight tenderness when I tapped my forehead and under my eyes, and it wasn't because I was tapping myself too hard. The uneasy tension traveled to my chest, and as I continued to tap I could feel my body tensing up, and then, all at once, quickly becoming more relaxed.

Tapping goes something like this:

1. First, identify the fear or the negative emotion that you want to release.

2. Second, tap the outside of your hands gently while using an "anchor" idea or message to release the fear from your mind. For example, if you've identified that you are afraid of the results of a recent medical exam, you can use the following message as an anchor: "Even though I'm not sure what the results of the tests will be, I let go of the fear that I'll get bad news, and I accept myself fully and completely, just the way I am."

3. Next, move to the forehead, right above your eyebrows, using your index and middle fingers.

4. Then move to the upper lip, under your nose.

5. Then under your lips, on the chin.

6. Then tap on your chest while you repeat the same messages out loud.

7. Finally, tap yourself under one armpit, repeating the anchor message.
8. To close the first round of tapping, move on to the top of your head and keep repeating the anchor message.
9. Take a deep breath, then repeat the process with one more round of tapping.

This is a quick version of how to tap, but there are plenty of resources online that can help you learn the techniques at home. Experts suggest that you close your eyes throughout the exercise so that you can feel a deeper mind–soul connection. Interestingly enough, I only started closing my eyes a few days after I began tapping, I guess because it was when I started to feel the difference in my mind and in my body that I was able to trust that the exercise would really work. It doesn't surprise me that it took me a minute to get used to closing my eyes. After all, it is in my nature to question things, to inquire, to make sure that I can anticipate the result of my every action. The planner, the control-minded personality, shows up even when I'm trying to soothe myself down.

Experts in the field of tapping agree that a person will start feeling relief from their symptoms fairly quickly, even after the two rounds of tapping. They suggest that one continue with this therapy for at least thirty days to alleviate emotions surrounding a special situation or emotion that one wants to release.

Others argue that the results are temporary. I've seen positive results when I tap myself and I'm convinced that it has had a positive impact that has helped keep my anxiety under control. In fact, I've tapped myself in the middle of breakdowns when I feel like I'm about to burst into tears over a situation. It might seem "woo-woo" for some, but I found that the science behind it makes lots of sense. So why not try it?

I've taken things a step further. I'm trying to get Lucian to try it too! In fact, I'm trying to get him to like not only tapping but also affirmations.

A few months ago, at 6:45 on a bright early morning, I was standing in front of the sink in my son's bathroom. I was teaching him how to have a morning self-pep-talk, and I suggested that he try tapping. I didn't know of any empirical data about the benefits of tapping in young children, but I figured it couldn't hurt to try, as it feels like you are massaging your body in a special way. I suggested that Lucian take a few minutes every morning to look at himself in the mirror and repeat words of encouragement that could help him through the day. I even tapped in front of him, and he looked at me and said, "Mom, that's weird." We both laughed.

In the world of mindfulness, using words of encouragement or affirmations is a very popular technique in the treatment of certain mental illnesses. Louise Hay first came up with this concept, and ever since it's been used by therapists who work with children and adults suffering from low self-esteem, depression or anxiety. I ask Lucian if he ever feels stressed about an upcoming test. And is there a performance or soccer game coming up that can be making him nervous? The answer is usually a flat "no." But, I figure, maybe my son can benefit from knowing these techniques, just in case.

When I was growing up, my mom had basically one recipe to dissolve any stress or worry that might have been bothering us: prayer. I'm not sure that it worked all the time, but I've continued to pray when I'm feeling overwhelmed. My friend Elisa says she prays too, when she is feeling the same way. I hope that Lucian can also find solace in prayer as he grows older.

Regardless of the situation, I remind Lucian that in the mornings he should look at himself in the mirror and recognize how wonderful a little boy he is. I ask him to talk to himself with suggested messages to reinforce self-acceptance.

THE HEALTH FREAK

○ While I'm not a "foodie," I can appreciate a great meal. I'm not going to lie; I grew up eating the most organic food you can imagine. My grandma in Arecibo used to get her poultry from the farmers market, and milk was delivered to her doorstep. Those were the days. I grew up with chickens in our backyard, and my mom would have us go collect the eggs from our own hens. The eggs were still warm when we'd pick them up.

As hard as it is for my son to eat his broccoli, he knows that unless he eats the vegetable on his plate he will not enjoy his favorite Popsicle after dinner. The truth is that some foods will help increase the mental health of our children as well as their physical health. Foods that contain coconut oil, fish oil, and protein, such as eggs, are especially helpful. Regardless of how calm we are as parents, when a child is hungry or when he is not well-nourished, he can be angry and uncooperative.

THE FRIEND

❂ Moms need time away from their family so that they can recharge. They need time to let loose and have regular woman-to-woman conversations, "breathing spaces" that allow them to share what they're feeling with those who very well may be going through similar circumstances. Sharing time with girlfriends should not only be about sharing problems, but also celebrating successes, even small ones, with people who genuinely care.

My much-needed girl time would not be possible without the support of my extended family. Since my divorce, I've been lucky to have kept a close bond with Lucian's grandparents. Their love for my son is a treasure that I never take for granted. Lucian's drawings tell the story of his love affair with Abuela Charlotte and Tata Alexander. In the family pictures you can always find Mom, Dad, Grandma, Grandpa, and the rabbit. Lucian is blessed to have these two wonderful people in his life. They are there at every major event, and they are always paying attention to areas that need to be addressed, always willing to lend a hand and always ready to spoil the boy just a tiny bit. The gift of loving grandparents in our children's lives is a treasure.

Aunties and uncles play a big part in that support system, too. Like my Aunt Estella for me, Lucian's favorite Auntie Catherine is a darling to him. And though all his uncles and aunties can't be around Lucian as often as they would like, their love and support have helped this anxious mom during times of stress, simply by checking in, by sending a card or a text message. Showing that one cares for the family is so important.

In my dealing with anxiety, I've learned to identify patterns and ways in which other relationships can be affected by it. While I've focused on the effects that anxiety can have at home, I am fully aware of the negative impact that my anxious moments have had on my interactions with friends and family. Luckily for me, I've easily shared my struggles with my family throughout these past few years, and when there have been disagreements (and we all know that there are sometimes tense moments between family members), I've learned to take responsibility for my share. Apologizing is not easy, but I've had to apologize for my actions, anxiety aside, when I've been out of control or simply too stressed to be careful about my choice of words.

I'm now more cognizant of my thought processes and of the assumptions that I sometimes make because of overthinking. Where I used to share my thoughts and opinions freely and at times carelessly, I am now more aware of the images that come up in my head and the words that I choose to define them.

Acting on impulse and learning how to control our emotions is a topic that I often talk about with my young son. It's something that can negatively affect our relationships with friends, family, and even those at work. Wherever we carry our thoughts, we have to be vigilant. It sounds like hard work, but with time one gets used to slowing things down, mentally speaking. It's easy to be judgmental and opinionated with our own family, because we assume, at the end of the day, they will be there for us. Yet, especially with the elders in my family, I try to be more patient.

Allowing the person next to you to simply "be" is sometimes hard for an anxious mom, or an anxious friend like me.

The ideas above are geared toward the child, and they all boil down to being more present in our interactions with our children, with our family, and with others. Never before have people spent so much time on the internet, and never before have parents been so distracted by social media platforms. Facebook, meant to be an outlet for college students, has now become a place where millions of parents and grandparents meet to share their stories of the day, pictures of their lovelies, and news, or simply to connect with their peers.

The popularity of social media platforms has become a challenge for parents, as they want to manage the amount of time their children spend online; but if we thought these platforms presented a problem for children and young adults, we ought to think again.

Adults spend hours in front of their screens scrolling Facebook, giving likes to the world and posting images to let the world know how wonderful their life is. In reality, most people browse their social media pages out of boredom. If you are a parent who spends hours on your cell phone browsing pages without a reason, consider taking a conscious break from technology.

TAKE A BREAK FROM THE WEB

A strategy to help you become that teacher that you are meant to be for your child is to be more present, engage in more activities that promote meaningful conversations, and create calmness around your child:

⚙ **Meet with nature**: The go-to source of inspiration for writers since the beginning of time has been going to meet nature. It's the easiest way to leave your worries behind and recharge. I love going to the park and watching children play, and I've taken Lucian to numerous parks around our area through the years. Discovering new things, touching the leaves of plants, and smelling flowers encourages them to appreciate the details around them, and this will lead a more joyful life.

When Lucian is at a park, surrounded by nature, I notice that he starts creating games of his own. He giggles, he smiles, he bursts into laughter. It seems that being around nature helps him come up with new ideas, creating new images of worlds to be explored.

When I notice the sense of wonder in his eyes, it's a wonderful time to connect with Lucian and to help him understand the world around him. His questions, which can be many, give me the chance to explain things in a way that he can understand.

I make an effort to have him stay away from the electronics because I feel that, instead, he could be coming up with clever new ways of building his Legos or drawing a picture of his favorite book characters. If we encourage them to spend more time in unstructured games, we will be allowing them to develop new ideas, and through this process they will learn more about what makes them happy.

⚙ **Words of encouragement**: The weight that our words have on our children can't be underestimated. Children look up to us for everything, from learning how to eat their meals to learning how to conduct conversations with friends, to helping resolve disagreements with their classmates. What we say and how we say it will have a lasting impression on their small minds. Experts point out also the impact that gestures, even the faces we make as parents when we reprimand them as toddlers, can have an impact on the way they perceive acceptance about who they are. Have you caught yourself being a little too angry when reprimanding your toddler?

My mom has reminded me of how stern my look can be when I'm mad. That is the kind of observation that you can't get from anyone else other than someone who knows you and cares about you deeply. She asked me one time to be aware of how I look when I'm reprimanding my son.

How I look? I was confused about her request. But when I thought about it more carefully, I understood. When I'm upset, I may be making a face that can scare my son. My face tenses, the lines in my forehead show up, I frown, and when I do this I'm not pleasant to look at.

When Lucian was a toddler, it was so hard not to scream when he colored the wall of the closet with crayons, or when he placed stickers on his bedroom furniture. Every time, I tried to remind myself that it was not the end of the world. Things are just that, things. Even the most valuable of our belongings, like laptops. Lucian once spilled orange juice over my laptop and it cost me a lot of money to get it repaired. It was a nightmare.

But however pricey the damage, however annoying the situation, my child needs to know that my love and acceptance are unconditional.

If I'm not careful with the words or the tone of voice I use when I reprimand Lucian, I may hurt his feelings and give him a reason to feel anxious around me. His heart is so tender, I could cause him to fear that he is not being accepted fully by his mother.

○ **Mindfulness techniques for children:** A new concept for many parents, promoting mindfulness in our children can help them understand that they can move beyond a moment of fear into a moment of calm and peace. Throughout the years, I've learned from numerous resources, including therapy and mindfulness books for children. These principles promote that a child can become attentive to the words he uses, that he can become aware of his thoughts, and that he can be comfortable with silence.

I've met therapists and teachers who have suggested ideas to help my son deal with fear. In those moments when he is afraid, we can put into practice the games and therapies that help him let go of fearful thoughts.

I've made it a priority to take time to meditate with my son, and I hope that as he grows older he will find value in meditation. For now I am trying to teach him about the benefits of silence and breathing softly. This is the one practice that I feel has most helped me deal with anxiety. But not just with anxiety—it also helps me clear my head when I'm feeling tired. The exercise can help our children get clear from thoughts of worry and help them find more energy inside their bodies.

If you haven't tried meditating with your child, try it and see how you feel afterwards. This is what meditating looks like:

You sit comfortably with your child in a quiet place, palms face up, and you begin to breathe slowly, taking a deeper breath in and out every time. Focusing on the breath is the key part of this exercise. Experts say that even a five- to ten-minute session once a day can help children feel calmer.

- **Family dinners**: "A family that eats and prays together, stays together," my mom would say often when we were growing up. I've heard this saying so many times, and while it sounds beautiful, I'm not sure that every family can actually pray and eat together all the time. The three of us kids would normally be outside in the front yard playing with our neighbors when we'd hear Mom's voice calling from the kitchen. We'd run inside to get ready for dinner, my dad always at the head of the table. I wish more families could do just that; if not praying together, and even without the dad at the head of the table, at least eating together and not in front of the TV.

  Sitting with the family around the table for regular meals encourages our children to learn about each other's day. Especially when you meet up at the table at the end of the week, you can plan ahead, share ideas of events that the children could take advantage of, and compare the calendar of activities so that everyone in the family understands what the days ahead will look like.

☼ **Going on a date**: Parents often try to make time to have a date night with their partners, and I think that is a wonderful idea. Nurturing the bond between spouses and getting away from the children, if only for a few hours, is a healthy thing. It forces us to switch gears and remember what it felt like to be an adult having an adult conversation with our spouse, ideally without mentioning the children too much. Similarly, one-on-one dates with our children are a great way to connect with them. When the activities of the week don't allow us to come to a calming place with our children, maybe scheduling a one-on-one date can give us the opportunity to do something special that they enjoy; go to the movies, for ice cream or for a hot dog at their favorite restaurant.

☼ **Positive self-talk:** Positive talk aimed at ourselves is the first step in breaking away from negative, anxiety-ridden thoughts. When you are a happy woman you are a happy mom, so once you've gotten your own mood in check you can then help your child engage in self-talk.

I've asked Lucian to look at himself in the mirror while he brushes his teeth. "I love myself," is what I've suggested that he say. Admittedly, he has looked at me kind of funny, but I remind him that it's a good time to appreciate everything about himself, from the brown curly hair to the mole above his lip to the eyeglasses that help him see the world more clearly. He gets an advantage if he sets himself up with the right attitude. The right attitude starts with loving every part of himself.

- **Pet your pet**: There is a calming effect in petting our pets. These days I try to take my time when I pet our rabbit, Fluffy. I look at her, I talk to her. I notice that she enjoys it and I do too. I've found myself asking Lucian to take his time when he pets our rabbit. It shouldn't be another chore around the home, but a time to enjoy the company of this pet that he chose. I remind Lucian of our responsibility to care for Fluffy, and I encourage him to acknowledge her when he comes into the room. Even his "Hi, Fluffy" in a less-than-excited tone will do the trick. The idea is to teach Lucian that his pet also needs love and attention.

- **Plant a flower:** When Lucian was a toddler, he used to love playing with dirt. Now he doesn't want to come close to the plants because he doesn't want to get dirty. However, I've found that Lucian enjoys helping me water the plants or do other chores around the house. Sometimes I'm planting flowers and I offer a small reward. He doesn't engage as much because of his dislike of dirt, but the moments that we spend together choosing the flowers and bringing them home are very special to me, and I hope that in the future he can have the memory of helping mom around the house, even if playing gardener is not on his list of favorite things to do.

All of the above are good tips that moms can choose to practice with their little ones, but there is not a one-size-fits-all approach to creating a special place of calmness around your child. Each individual parent will know which ideas will apply best to their family and to their lifestyle. If I could boil down the tips and advice for helping moms to release their anxiety, I would say slow down, be more attentive, be more present, and be a better listener.

There are days when I listen to Lucian intently, when I feel like I'm focused and I can tackle any topic. And every question of his that comes my way is a topic that we can discuss without rush. Those days, I feel like someone waiting for the climax of a movie to unfold. I realize that my son is experiencing so many things for the first time in his life, and I want to participate. I want to be the first one to hear about his new adventures, to observe the things around him the same way that he does with the hope that I can understand him better. Because being a good communicator means that we must listen attentively to the other person, I try to remind myself that I don't need to tell Lucian things as much as to listen. I should also do more asking than telling.

I want to teach my son over time about the importance of finding comfort in silence. Lately, I've gotten in the habit of playing a meditation recording for him when it's time to go to sleep. He is seeing how quickly he falls asleep, and for that I'm grateful, for at least through these meditations he can keep away the monsters that come from under the bed or the wolves that come across our backyard to threaten our pet.

If I can't teach anything else to my son, I want him to understand that he has the tools to face his fears in life. He alone can pull himself out of situations that might cause him to be afraid, as he is a perfectly equipped little boy.

8

Ahead of the Wave

⌒‿

Healing comes through true connections.

— Jeremy R. Geffen

I t's May 2018 and the allergy season in Georgia is about to end. Pollen is the main culprit during this time of the year. It is beautiful to see the new colors of the flowers in bloom, but the inescapable dust covers every surface, from patio furniture to the front steps of your home to the top of your car. Even if it's sitting in the parking lot for only a couple of hours, you'll be guaranteed to find a film of a yellow dust covering the whole car.

Pollen was just as bad this year as last year, and Lucian has reacted just as badly to the unfriendly visit of our friend the pollen. While allergy medications seem to help, it often takes a multi-prong approach to protect him. His eyes, especially, get extremely irritated, and if I don't help prevent it, the scratching can cause an irritation in the membranes of his eyes so severe that he ends up with conjunctivitis. It has happened before to many children at school, and this year the principal has allowed children to wear baseball caps so that they can keep the pollen off their faces as much as possible.

The morning ritual during this time of the year is more rigorous, as we need to make time to get Lucian's allergy medication by mouth, as well as eye drops and nasal spray. The evening ritual is not much different, except that he also needs to be sure to wash his hair every night to get the pollen out of it. His face can get bloated with pollen within a couple of hours. One evening about a year ago, we had arrived home and I had asked Lucian to wash his face to clean away the pollen. Two hours later, as we were getting ready to go to sleep, I noticed his eyes were red and swollen and he was so uncomfortable.

"I was afraid to tell you, Mom. I thought you'd be mad at me."

I was sitting on the edge of his bed as Lucian was quietly telling me this. I noticed that as he spoke, his body was hunched over, and he was looking down and lowering his head as if acknowledging that he had made a terrible mistake.

The disciplinarian in me was at odds with the warmer and gentler side of me. While I wanted my son to follow instructions and listen to his mother's advice, I never wanted him to feel that he needed to be afraid.

That moment reminded me of the times when I'd given advice to my son but he decided to ignore it or simply forgot. I fear that if he ignores my advice now, something more serious than a set of swollen eyes might result. I think about lessons that I must impart in the years ahead so that I can help Lucian stay safe. Will I be there with him at all times to protect him from all illnesses? No. Will my advice stay with him so that he can act in ways that will keep him out of danger?

I realize that during this age, Lucian needs a certain level of "helicopterism" from me. However strict I might think I am, I recognize that there are times when I haven't been the best parent, when I have forgotten to pay more attention, when I have been impulsive and reacted without really being careful of the consequences of my decisions, and now that Lucian is older I can see that I've slowly gained the "hang" of things. If I slow down, I can be a better listener. If I pay more attention, I can help seed messages that can remind Lucian of who he is, so that he can face the challenges that will come in the years ahead. I've been guilty of missing the point, of jumping into a conversation, of interrupting him when he was so excited to tell me about something that happened at school.

The other day, for example, as I picked him up from the after-school program, his face looked a bit sad. I asked, as I normally do, "How was your day?"

It only took a second for him to start listing the number of things that had gone wrong during this day:

1. He had hit a friend in the face with a ball, but it was an accident.
2. His friend then told another friend, who in turn got mad at Lucian.
3. The two friends started calling Lucian names and making fun of him.
4. One of them took the glasses off Lucian's face and threw them to the ground.
5. Lucian told his teacher, but according to Lucian his teacher just casually told the boys, "Hey, play nice."

For the next twenty minutes, Lucian told me how terrible this day had been for him. In fact, it had been the "worst" day for him. These days, the situation plays out differently than it would have three or four years ago. These days, kids don't just laugh at my child, like that time in the park.

Lucian laid out the scenario in full detail as we hopped in the car. As I was driving, I tried to offer words of wisdom that could help my child feel better about the situation that he so passionately described. Where his tone was desperate, I was faring well, I stayed calm. When he seemed to be puzzled by the actions of others, I reminded him that it's better to ignore the bad behavior than to join in and react in a negative way. When he couldn't understand *why* the kids acted the way they did (grabbing his eyeglasses and throwing them to the ground), I reminded him that in life there will be many wonderful people who will bring fun times, but there will also be some who are not kind. His job: ignore. Tell the teacher, walk away.

I explained the concept of "offering an olive branch" to Lucian so that he could also consider this when dealing with arguments with his friends at school. I tried to keep things simple for him: ignore the bad behavior, talk to the teacher in charge, remove yourself from a dangerous situation.

When it comes to social skills development for my son, I'm very good at letting him deal with the situation on his own, without my help. I want to provide guidance for Lucian and protect him at all times, but I realize that I'm not going to be there all the time. What will happen if he becomes too dependent on an adult saving him when he and his friends get into an argument?

Lucian has had to learn the hard way that as he grows up an only son, he might be on his own a lot—when he goes to the playground or when he is at the after-school program, or even when we go on vacation. There are times when he will have to face situations without an older brother or sister around to stand by his side. Therefore, he needs to have the tools to try to defend himself from any dangerous situation. It is when he is faced with difficult circumstances that he will learn how to resolve conflicts that may arise around him.

The environment around our children is constantly changing, I'm aware of this, and therefore I must adapt my style of parenting to the current realities that Lucian faces, for example, making sure that he is able to manage the increasingly stressful environments around him.

The increase in gun violence at schools across the country has changed my perception of school as a safe environment for my son. That topic alone can get my anxious brain running at a hundred miles per hour. My compulsive set of thoughts gets stirred up inside, and my peaceful, Zen, hopeful moments of tranquility are turned upside down. I try to think of messages that I can seed so he can feel that he is safe, even when I'm not there to protect him.

I'm glad that I'm available to listen to my son when he has had a hard day. I can't help but think that hopefully he will not have too many hard days at this young age, but I want him to know that as years go by he can come to me with any concern and any worry that he might have. I don't want him ever to think that he can't tell me how he's feeling because he's afraid of how I'll react. I know that my duty as a parent is to be more attentive, to listen more carefully, and to check in with his teachers more frequently to make sure that Lucian's concerns on a bad day don't become a trend. In doing so, I can anticipate issues that might arise around him, and I might be able to prepare and have answers for the concerns and issues that will come as my son gets older. I must stay current with life's troubles and the many challenges that he will no doubt encounter as he learns to navigate the fragility of this existence.

The cyber effect of things is another area that worries this anxious mom. I find myself thinking a lot about the future these days. Lucian will soon start third grade, and we have so many years ahead before he goes off into the "real world" as an adult. Yet it seems that the future of things is reaching our children at an earlier age, and that worries me a lot. In this day and age, children are exposed to so much information, and not all of it is easy to digest, even for adults. I try to explain things to Lucian in the simplest of ways, but there are things that even I don't know how to explain.

How will I be able to control the access to technology when everyone around my son is allowing technology to take a more important role in their children's lives? I recently suggested to a mom that we should collectively decide when we will allow our children to access social media, for example. "Let's agree on what age they'll be when they can go on Facebook."

I'm adamant about the idea that we have to keep an eye on our children's use of technology, or the overuse of technology, for that matter. Children these days have iPhones when they are eight, and even YouTube channels by age nine. Before we as parents even become aware, our children may be learning about the latest naughty song that someone was watching somewhere around them. The music on the radio can have phrases that promote violence, and even social media in a few short years will be something that as a parent I will have to monitor very closely. While I'm concerned about the excess of information that might not be age-appropriate for my son, I must admit that there are yet other concerns that bother this anxious mother.

CHILDHOOD FRIENDS

Will I be able to offer the right balance in making sure that Lucian has a healthy social life and strong academic development? Am I allowing him enough unstructured time to play with his friends? Will he feel that he has enough support from friends at school? Will he be able to create friendships that last a lifetime? What about future friends? Will he be wise when choosing friends online when he gets old enough to engage in social media platforms?

Sophia's daughter Camila was my childhood friend and neighbor growing up, and we are very close to this day. She lived three houses from me. Sophia and my mom were pregnant at the same time, which I believe makes us technically sisters. Camila and I developed a different sort of friendship as we grew older; we attended the same high school, but we had somewhat different tastes and interests. She was more of an introvert when she was young, and she liked biology and chemistry, while I was the extrovert who liked to be a social butterfly. We seemed like opposites—I was an extrovert, she was more quiet, I would move fast, and she was more methodical—yet the bond we had had since childhood was unbreakable. I don't talk to Camila often, but when I do I feel that I'm going back in time, that we are the two girls who used to play on the beach together, ride our bikes down the street from our home, play with our dolls, and talk for hours about big dramas at school, the friends that were "mean" or "not nice," or the boys that we were secretly in love with.

Over the years we've had conversations about everything, from politics to parenting. We share each other's experiences and look for advice from each other, even if we have different perspectives. We are different in many ways, but the fact that we grew up in the same town and went to the same school, and the fact that I know her family and she knows mine, makes it easy for us to understand each other. Without saying much, we can go right there in a minute, and we understand where the other one is coming from—completely. Forty years later, we are still the closest of friends. Camila is the kind of person who will let you know exactly how she feels, and because she and I feel like we are almost sisters, I find that her opinions ring true for me, not just because they are based on her experience in life, but because they are rooted in our common experience as children.

We've learned to appreciate the differences in our personalities, and I can see a lot of great qualities in her that maybe I couldn't appreciate in the past. The wonderful thing about this friendship is that it has shown me how very different friends can teach you so much in life. Which makes me wonder, will my son Lucian have a friendship like this in his life?

The words of experts that remind us of the importance of providing the right balance in terms of social interaction for our children can't be overlooked. Finding the right balance between my son's time playing outside and his time of access to his tablet is something that I've struggled with. Because he is an only child, sometimes he doesn't have anyone else to play with. This is one of the reasons I regularly visit parks near our home. I like the idea that when he goes to the park, he can play with other children. But I realize that playing in the park will eventually not seem as exciting to him. In a few years, I'll be worrying more about other types of activities that he will prefer. For example, he might want to play with electronics more often. Balancing outside playtime with electronics playtime can be hard.

My concern over Facebook and other social media networks that are yet to develop is something that I want to continue monitoring, and as Lucian grows up I realize that his tendency to participate and engage in social media networks might expose him to a lot more than meets the eye.

> Having secrets is natural for a child. Snooping and spying on their online lives—pouncing on their unattended cell phone to read their texts or checking their social media activity is problematic. Studies show that children who have overbearing parents just learn to be more secretive. Worse than that, research shows that when those children run into trouble, the last people they will turn to are their overcontrolling parents. In other words, be vigilant, not vigilante.

This advice from Dr. Mary Aiken in *The Cyber Effect* is a hard pill to swallow, especially for an anxious mom like me. I look ahead at the years to come and realize that I will have to continue working on my balancing act: to exert influence and control but not to be too controlling, too overprotective, too ... anything.

Being comfortable with uncertainty has never been my forte, but I realize the wheels will certainly come off at some point or another. As I've learned, and as with many things in life, we learn how to cope, we heal and we move along. Over the past few years, I've become more aware of the need to address my anxiety, and I've felt that I'm reaching a point where I can be in control. Regardless of the situation, I will be able to manage it, and survive it, and move along.

What does the future hold for me and for Lucian? I can't tell for sure. What I do know is that I can't become overly comfortable with the label of "anxious mom" because there is a next phase for my relationship with my son. I'm graduating from anxious mommy school. I feel that we've entered a new phase, and because Lucian is older, he can now let me know how he feels, his words guiding me at times, in ways that I didn't know were possible. I must remain flexible and I shouldn't anticipate, but I must be prepared for the years ahead.

First and second grade have brought an easier rhythm to things. As Lucian has become more independent, I've learned to get my anxious mom tendencies under control and to anticipate the needs of my son. While staying on top of the school calendar can be a challenge, I am ready for stressful times during the year:

- Beginning of the school year
- End of semester
- Holiday season
- Family vacation

Being prepared reminds me of my mom's favorite advice: "Be prepared." It can help our children face their challenges. A five-year-old might be feeling nervous about joining a school performance and standing in front of his classmates. A nine-year-old might be facing a lot of stress because of homework or as she studies for a test. At 12, she is having frequent meltdowns about feelings of being ignored by her best friend at school, and at 15 she may feel that she doesn't have enough friends on social media.

"Lucian, do you prefer that Mommy cuddles with you at night and reads a book before you go to sleep? Or do you prefer to color with Mom?"

"I prefer to color with you."

My son is growing. He no longer prefers that I hug and kiss him like he used to. Instead, he enjoys sitting down and painting pictures using his imagination. Secretly, I'm always hoping that Lucian includes me in his picture.

As I work to alleviate the stress that anxiety can cause at times in my life, I try to be mindful and remind myself that Lucian's needs will change with time. What works today to create a calming environment may not work a year from now or even six months from now. When you have established a rhythm, it will take less energy to go back and fall into the habit of remaining calm under the circumstances, sharing your concerns with your child, taking time to check and get a pulse on what you feel might be a stressful time.

"There it is! Mom to the rescue!" I let loose a loud clap in the middle of my living room. I'm halfway through reading one of my favorite memoirs so far: *The Wishing Year*. I'm embroiled in Noelle's story of trying to make things happen in her life; buying a house is upon her if only she can gather the down payment needed to pay for this home in California. She tells the story of how, one day, she received a call from her mom in Italy, who explained that she had some money in a savings account that she had forgotten about, and she wanted to offer it so that Noelle could buy her first home.

I laughed out loud once more. The book had taken me to the point of loving profusely the idea of wishing and hoping that your most sacred desires can come true and being skeptical about ideas of magic and all things in between. This time I'm in, truly connected to the author's experience.

I've been there myself. My mom has saved me more than once. The author wonders about the help that she received when she most needed it: "Is this how it feels when wishes come true?" she asks. Which got me thinking about the many times since my divorce that my mom has been there for me—emotionally, financially, spiritually. I can relate to the feeling of uneasiness, the guilt trip that doesn't let you receive openly and willingly any present that your parents might offer. She has lent me money, many times sending presents, all without expecting anything in return. However, there is still a feeling of not being good enough. I want to pay my mom back for everything that she has done for me and my son.

Someday I want to take my mom to Israel. A devout Christian, Catholic to the core, my mom embodies the values that I want to pass on to my young son.

She wasn't the chatty type, my mom, but she was there. Always there, always present. She was raised in a different time and she is admittedly a shy personality. I know that on many occasions she would have wanted to address things differently. We have had long conversations and short ones that explode into arguments when we disagree. Somehow, however, as we've gotten older, we've learned to meet each other at a place where we can respect who each has become.

"Parents must learn to accept their children for who they are, not what the parents had hoped they would be."

— Sal Severe

I find such profound truth in this statement, but I realize how difficult it is not to expect so much; or should we as parents expect nothing from our children? How can we go through life not expecting a specific turnout for our child? Is that even possible?

In delving deeper, I realize that hope, like our fears, can play games with our minds. We *hope* for a bright future, we *hope* that our children are safe from harm, we *hope* that they grow up to become strong, healthy and happy. We hope. The act of hoping is like the act of wishing. And I'm not sure that I understand very well the difference between wishing and hoping for things to turn out the way I'd like them to. I keep ruminating over the analysis of this question. However, I am aware that I'd be placing a heavy burden on my child if I expected him to become something that I've fabricated, the perfect life that I think he must have.

But what is the perfect life-path? Is it a long life, full of laughter, of friendships that last a lifetime, of health that springs from a strong body and mind? Do I want my child to be successful? And what does success mean? This is the very question that we as adults are still trying to answer even decades after graduating from high school, after college degrees and marriages, or failed marriages, after careers that are challenging and fulfilling and jobs that are boring but pay handsomely and those that don't. What is the picture that I want to paint for my son as he grows older and meets life's countless challenges?

"Mommy, Mommy!"

On a gloomy afternoon a few years ago I was sitting at a park close to our home while Lucian was playing. Suddenly, he came running toward me, sobbing profusely. Most of the children at the playground that day had left, and only three remained. A bit older, they were standing under the bridge in between the slides.

Lucian's eyes were red, his face wet from tears. "Those kids were making fun of me, Mommy!"

I heard laughter in the background, and as I looked more closely, I saw two older boys and a girl standing there looking at us. They must have been about three years older than Lucian.

They seemed to be laughing among themselves as they looked away, trying to hide their faces. I could've jumped over the red fence and punched them. Instead, I turned to my young son and hugged him.

"I'm sorry, Lucian. Don't pay attention to those kids."

"They're mean, Mommy!"

From where I was standing, I couldn't see what went on and to this day I don't know exactly what happened, but remembering the face of my son as he ran to my arms looking for protection had me thinking that I had better trust. I'd better trust heavily and deeply that something, somewhere, will protect my son wherever he goes, because as much as I wish I could be right there to open my arms and hold him when a mean boy comes his way, I will not always be there. And so I will have to trust. I will have to trust in God and the angels above, the Universe or the divine order of things to keep my child safe, at least until I'm buried a few feet down so that I can be spared seeing him suffer. Ever. I tell myself that he will be okay, that he will be protected. In my head, I have a conversation going again, and I find myself contradicting the very things that I want Lucian to believe.

"You are always safe, always protected."

But is he? Will I be able to impart teachings that will protect him from the real mean kids that he will one day face in this world?

"If only things could stay the way they were."

It's what I say when I miss my neighbors. We underestimate the value of neighbors. In our efforts to live lives of independence, we seldom stop and say hello to those closest to us. I grew up playing with neighbors, down the street from my home. Lucian hasn't had the same experience, and sometimes I wonder if this is something that he'll miss having in life: neighbors and other kids to play with. We used to have three families in our neighborhood with children around Lucian's age; the kiddos would meet at the cul-de-sac and the moms would sit on a corner and chat. It was a beautiful life, I remember thinking. If only I could take a break from work and sit down every afternoon while Lucian plays in the street.

And I did, shortly thereafter. I was again without a job, but I really was loving the experience of being free every afternoon so that I could watch Lucian play outside. The kids would attempt to ride their bicycles or go racing in their three-wheelers, laughter illuminating their faces. Until of course one of them would trip and fall.

The moms on my street were the nicest ones. We'd plan for "kids night" at the restaurant nearby and take the kiddos for a movie and dinner. It was a fun time. Two years later most of the neighbors had moved away, and Lucian would often ask, "Can we go visit?" Life gets in the way sometimes, yet I still cherish those years when Lucian could experience exactly what I experienced when I grew up.

Connecting is important, especially connecting beyond school recess; "unstructured play," as the teacher calls it. Lucian is an expert at making up games and I encourage it. I can only hope that I'm not too protective, or too worried about what might happen as the games start to change. A few years ago he was riding a simple tricycle; now he's riding a bike, and next year it will be a skateboard and then I'll be losing my mind with concern over what could happen to this child of mine as he ventures off into the world.

The exercise of looking ahead at what the world might hold for my son can cost me dearly.

"You have a really vivid imagination," Lucian's therapist would tell him as he tried to come up with ideas that would calm Lucian's fears when he went to bed at night.

For me, real anxiety can kick in if I let my mind run wild with ideas of what Lucian's future will look like. Will he do well at school, will he thrive in middle school, will he have a knack for algebra, what about chemistry? Will he graduate and go to college? If so, which college? Will he want to leave town and leave his mom behind like I wanted to do when I was in high school? Here we go again.

Looking ahead at what the future might hold for me or for Lucian is not a practice that helps me stay calm. I make every effort to go against my nature of being a dreamer sometimes. I know I must limit the amount of time that I daydream of the future, because I know that the most important moment is happening now. I should focus on the *now* and not on the future. I breathe deeply and try to stay in the realm of this day, of this very moment. I revisit the pages of one of my favorite books, *The Power of Now*, when I need a reminder of the principles that can help me stay on track. Eckhart Tolle's most illuminating words bring me back to a place of calm: "All negativity is caused by an accumulation of psychological time and denial of the present. Unease, anxiety, stress, tension, worry—all forms of fear—are caused by too much future, and not enough present.

"In the Now, in the absence of time, all your problems dissolve. Suffering needs time; it cannot survive in the Now."

As I meditate, I see myself in front of the fallen trees, the roots exposed and dried out from the heat of the sun. It's a hopeless view from here, except for the fact that other trees around the fallen ones are cooking up a comeback.

I travel back in time for a moment, and I remember that visit to my mom when I smashed her new car against the wall. It had been the first time I'd visited my mom in Puerto Rico since Hurricane Maria hit the island. On that trip, I experienced moments of anxiety because my mind was running wild with reasons to be worried. I was also excited to spend time with my family and especially my lovely niece, who was only about five months old at the time. While my strategies to fight anxiety were very much in place, I had my moments when the reality of the situation around us pushed my limits. Traffic lights were not working on some of the main roads of my hometown. The electricity was back on at my mom's house, but because of the extensive repairs that were being made to the grid across the island, sometimes the power went off unexpectedly. We call these "apagones," or blackouts, and those living in Puerto Rico know that apagones can happen often.

On one of the evenings during that visit we were sitting around the living room when suddenly the house went pitch dark. Lucian was terrified. He had never been in a situation like this before. Luckily, he was not alone. Luckily, power was back within the hour. But being there, sitting next to my son in a familiar place, having experienced blackouts throughout my childhood, I realized the power of the unexpected. I told my son not to be afraid. I was right there sitting next to him, even when he couldn't see me.

That night when the power went out I remained calm. Because I had remained calm the whole time, Lucian, after initially feeling afraid, was able to stay calm as well, even though he had never experienced a blackout.

This very notion of remaining calm and staying in the present moment is on the list of key principles that I want my son to carry with him: "You are not alone" and "Don't worry about tomorrow, focus on today."

So here is how I approach my son's fears: there are a few messages that I keep going back to while we are having breakfast or driving to school, before bedtime or over dinner. I try to seize every teachable moment when I can. As a mom, I feel the responsibility to go beyond my own fears and try to help Lucian face his fears.

TOOLS OF THE TRADE FOR MY SON

There are messages that I want Lucian to always remember when I'm not there with him. I like to think of them as tools or imaginary gadgets to trick his fear:

1. You are not alone. Wherever you go, my son, I am right there with you.

    His fear of being alone in his bedroom at night has gone on for a long time. One time we took Lucian to a hypnotherapist, and she had a tape made for him to help him go to sleep more easily. In this tape, the therapist suggested how he could build a force field around his bed and around his home to protect himself and his family from any strangers. Then she suggested how Lucian could give permission for his body to fall asleep, starting with his toes, moving on to his legs, then his belly, and so on. Before the tape was over, my son was sound asleep.

The practice has encouraged me to find yet other ways to help my son relax and slowly fall asleep. I suggest that you think of songs that are soothing and that can bring sweet memories to your child. I remember a song my mom used to sing to me that talked about a little boy who had a horse and was going to the city to help Sally when she was sick. The problem was that at the end of the song it said, "If you die, dear Sally, no worries, you'll go straight to heaven." I think my mom never intended for me to remember this particular song for the rest of my life, but I can recall not only the song, but also my mom's sweet voice. Yet I now look back and wonder why she chose this song. So, when I pick songs to sing to my child at night, I make sure that I stay in the relaxing, positive realm. You never know how lasting this memory will be.

"Find comfort in the dark, in the silence of the night, my son," I feel like saying to my sweet child, yet I know that for his young age, being alone at night in his room can trigger images of monsters or thunder or danger. I've taken to sleeping next to him until he falls asleep. I wonder when the time will come that I can stop this practice. Not every mom can afford to wait until her child falls asleep to leave the room, so I consider myself lucky that I'm able to do so. For now, I can patiently wait until he grows out of this fear.

2. You are equipped. Life will no doubt present you with tough lessons, with moments when you feel that you can't win, but trust that you have what it takes to make it.

From the stress of homework to the tension of standing in front of the class to talk about a school subject, you are well equipped to face the challenges ahead and fight them.

If you are an anxious mom like me, you'd like to be sure that your child will be safe everywhere he goes. It doesn't take a lot of imagination to be concerned about our children's safety. The increase in gun violence at schools in recent years has sharpened the fear of parents in the United States about a new type of danger that they and their parents could never have imagined. It takes only a few minutes of the news to make us understand that the world we live in can be a scary one. I've tried to explain the dangers of the world to my son, but I've not always wanted to paint the gruesome picture that would make him terrified of being alone. Perhaps I should. I try to remind him that no matter where he is, regardless of the circumstances, he is well equipped to remain calm amidst chaos.

I feel that this is an area that will take a lot of effort on my part in the years ahead, and I hope I can tackle each of my son's questions about fearful subjects with a sense of hope. We are all spiritual beings living a human experience, as Wayne Dyer would say. I would like my son to have the tools to face his fears and remain calm in the face of tragedy. I want him to know that there is a force that he can't see inside of him, ready to guide and strengthen him even when he might feel like he is lost.

3. "It's okay to fail sometimes. Regardless of how bad it looks right now, you can pass the key tests in your life."

Lucian loves soccer, and he is quite good at it. Ever since he was five, he would say, "I want to be a soccer player." However, three years later he might say, "I don't want to be a soccer player anymore." There are days when he loves the game and other days when he hates the effort that he needs to put forth in practice.

I would say that neither his mom nor his dad is a prolific sportsman, so initially I didn't know what to make of having an athletic child. Fortunately for us, we enjoy coming out to see him play on the weekends. Every time he scores, it's a major reason to celebrate. We go for pizza or an ice cream, we talk about how that amazing move that my son made at the very last minute was so fun to watch. The joy in Lucian's sweet face would last for days, just from thinking how he could score a goal.

I try to remind Lucian that winning can be more fun than losing, but that losing forces him to look back at a mistake and try to make it better the next time. More importantly, mistakes and disappointments can make him stronger and build his character.

Similarly, as a parent, I must be careful that I'm not projecting my own desires for a particular career, in sports or science or math or whatever, on my child. I must admit that I may be a victim of what is called "helicopterism," that is, hoping your child will succeed in a specific track so that he can follow a certain path career-wise. We call "helicopter moms" those that are always on top of their child's every activity. Beyond becoming a helicopter mom, there is risk of becoming a "tiger mom." A tiger mom is one who wants her child to succeed so much that she relentlessly pushes him or her to excel, often building a long list of activities and filling up the child's calendar for the whole week.

From sports activities to tutoring lessons to learning second languages, children often feel overwhelmed with the amount of activity their parents have lined up for them. In recent years, there has been a wave of opinion in favor of giving less homework to children. I'm not arguing for less homework, as in the end it's equally defendable to say that your child needs all the knowledge he can get because he will face fierce competition for jobs when he grows up. Yet children love to play, and it is through play that they learn more about their own preferences and strengths, and through unstructured games their social skills are developed. Moreover, the feelings of being overwhelmed with schoolwork can cause a child to develop anxiety, especially if they are not enjoying the activities to the fullest.

Between helicopterism and tigerism, if I let things get out of hand I can find myself having extremely high expectations for my child. I try to keep a certain balance as I approach activities for my child and my expectations. For example, given the preference, I would love it if my son continued playing soccer and became an accomplished athlete. But I have to stay open and accept his choices, and I will show him how proud I am if he decides to change his mind and choose another sport.

4. "You are protected. Even in the scariest of circumstances, know that you are protected by the divine."

I grew up in a religious family and have experienced religion as an important part of my value system; therefore, for me, prayer can be a meaningful resource to escape the madness of the week. Finding time to gather in a church can bring many benefits beyond the obvious one. Praying in and of itself forces anxious moms like me to be still and quiet. The task of being still and quiet can be challenging to many moms because we are so used to running around, checking our to-do lists, driving our children places, listening to the phone ringing (not just ours, but our kids' phones too!). Finding a quiet time to sit down and relax is good for us, and for our children.

I find that the greatest benefit of visiting a church or common space of worship is that we are faced with a simple but profound observation: we are not alone.

I am not alone when I'm worried about my parents falling ill. I am not alone when I think that a child might be hiding a deep fear from others. I am not alone when I feel that life's circumstances can be at times so overwhelming. I am not alone when I wish I could just check out for a few days and forget about long lists of things to do around the house: the laundry, the groceries, the planning of meals for the week, and on and on. When an anxious mom like me sits at church, it doesn't always mean that my mind will be put at ease. I might be sitting quietly while my mind is out for a ride, my thoughts going somewhere else. When I catch myself in this mode, I "come back."

I like sitting there among other moms with their families. I wonder how many of them are struggling. When I look around, I recognize that there is a special sense of community present there. That sense of community is much needed today. I have withdrawn from everyone, including my religion, to find clarity of mind, only to find myself years later rekindling my relationship with God and with my parish. I go back for moments of silence that have forced me to connect with others in a different way. While social media might seem to bring us a few hundred more friends to like online, sometimes the *depth* of friendship is lost. We can connect with others when we get closer. Joining others who might be facing similar challenges gives me a sense of community and helps my son feel that he belongs to a greater tribe than just his family.

I often glance at the idea of inviting fear into our lives. I hesitate. *Inviting fear into our lives sounds like going in the opposite direction, doesn't it?* I try to run away from my fears and find a shelter where I feel comfortable and safe.

When I think about tricking my fears, I feel empowered. I realize that I'm more than my fears, that I can control every thought and can manage my emotions in such a way that I can release any tension that can manifest because of fear, anxiety, and worry. I must be vigilant to recognize those moments when I can share this knowledge with my son. In times ahead he will be required to face his own fears. I trust that he will be ready.

9

Masters in Disguise

Listen to the child in you and follow its innocence.

– Munia Khan

What do I see when look into my son's eyes? Have I looked at him lately? I mean *really* looked at him? What do I see? Do I see a part of myself, or do I recognize the features from his dad that, together with mine, make Lucian unique? The broad bright smile, or the round brown eyes and curly brown hair that sometimes reminds me of my father. The uniqueness of that face is a mystery. How can my child be so perfect? I ask myself. Beyond his eyes and his words, there is a strong spirit that is showing his mom things she never knew before. His friends might also be able to see this lively spirit as well.

It's April 2018, and Lucian is eight years old, three months older than his best friend Neal (a fact that he likes to remind me of). "I will *always* be three months older than Neal."

The friendship of these two boys is one of a kind. Where Neal is methodical, Lucian is loose in his pattern of doing things. I watch them play with their Legos and am amazed at the difference in their ways of playing. Neal carefully reads every word in the booklet, following the steps closely. Meanwhile, Lucian spreads all the pieces in front of him and attempts to come up with his own creation, which doesn't always resemble what the booklet shows. Slowly, these two have developed their own dynamics; they are yin and yang. They go to the same school and are in the same classroom. His mom and I celebrated this when it was announced at the beginning of the year. Finally!

Like Lucian and Neal, my friend Elizabeth and I have a solid friendship. No doubt, our friendship has been a constant source of strength and support throughout these past seven years. With similar backgrounds and values, we've journeyed together through the past two decades. We both moved to Atlanta in our twenties in search of our dream career. We both married in our early thirties and had children in our late thirties. We are both bicultural and bilingual, and we both lost our dads when we were young. Friends like Elizabeth are hard to find. Even with the ups and downs along the way, we've managed to stick together. I met Elizabeth through an ex-boyfriend. Sadly, he had moved away and years later passed away after battling cancer. Although he and I didn't stay an "item," I thank him for the gift of this wonderful girlfriend.

We've been married and pregnant at the same time, Elizabeth and I. She with Neal and I with Lucian. We've seen each other through painful circumstances, and have had our differences, too. She has forgiven my anxiety modes more than once and has taught me areas where I can be more patient and less judgmental. When we get together, we tell ourselves that we'll be cleaning each other's butts when we are old ladies. I can picture that, even if I try not to.

Throughout the years that followed my divorce, I embraced many roles. While trying my best to be a better parent, I've become more of a teacher, a playmate, and a friend at times; a constant, consistent source of guidance.

I never thought I would describe myself as a teacher to my son. I didn't even think I would enjoy teaching anything to anyone, until this child became a toddler who would ask questions. I became eerily aware that with every answer to his questions I bore the responsibility of delivering information that was factual and true.

"Let's Google it, Lucian. Siri, show me a picture of a hare."

Ever since I got Lucian his pet rabbit, he has been obsessed with all things bunny. Fluffy is his only pet, and though mom takes care of her for the most part, Lucian is a proud "parent." She stood out from the rest of the bunnies the day that Lucian and I went to the pet store in the fall of 2014. Aside from the tones in her fur, I'm not sure what else stood out for Lucian on that day.

Going against the judgment of my son's dad, who had long warned me against getting any pets for Lucian ("It's a lot to handle," he'd say) I wanted my son to have the experience of caring for a pet. Sometimes pets can be our friend when no one else is around. Their energy is calming, and when we pet them after a long day, it feels like a reward.

Aside from giving my child a partner to play with, I've used the idea of having a pet to impart lessons that I feel can be useful in his young life. These lessons, I admit, come out of nowhere sometimes. They just appear before me, yet I like the way they turn out: compassion, for starters, and acknowledging the presence of someone in the room.

"Have you acknowledged Fluffy today, Lucian?"

The habitual tasks that come with having a rabbit, I can live without. Some days I want the years to go by quickly so that we get to the point when we have to kiss our rabbit goodbye. I even wonder how she will make her exit. Will she escape our home? An impossible proposition, since she lives comfortably in a six-by-two-foot cage and seems to be happy. So happy that even when I open the gate of her cage sometimes she refuses to get out. I have to talk her into stretching her legs, and sometimes I even have to pick her up and show her that it's okay to hop around the kitchen for a while.

"Come on, Fluffy. Come on out."

Outside of her cage, her tour around the kitchen has looked the same for years now. She hops quickly toward the storage bench across the kitchen and finds her favorite corner under the bench. The space is tight, and I guess she likes to rub her fur against the wood panel. She can stay under the bench for hours and if I let her, she will start gnawing away the wood underneath. It takes a few loud claps for her to get that she needs to stop the biting or she is going back inside the cage. She stays there for a minute, and if I'm not close enough to dissuade her from munching away the baseboards, she will add to the already long line of dented spots along the rim of the floor molding.

I've wondered how long we need to keep the rabbit. I've heard stories from friends who, upon being faced with the daily routine of cleaning up the stinky poops and smelly pee of their rodents, have decided to give the pets away. Some parents are more creative than others in arranging for their pet's disappearing act to rid them from their lives. I can't blame them. There are times when I daydream about the perfect way to rid myself of the daily chore. I imagine that I'm taking the cage downstairs for a good hose-down party and the bunny escapes to the wooded area behind our townhome. Or maybe I could be more careful than that and more civilized. I imagine myself reaching out to a bunny rescue center where they would take the bunny and find her a home. The idea that the bunny would end up in a new home seems more humane. And it would be better than the ends that my two bunnies had.

When I grew up, my mom reminds me, we didn't have one but two rabbits. I have very little memory of them hopping around the house, but I remember that they were gray. They lived in a large wire cage in our backyard and we'd go outside and pet them, and feed them with hay and rabbit food. I'm not sure how they "exited" my life. This not knowing what happened to my two bunnies is a topic of discussion with Lucian, who finds it disheartening. Even my mom can't explain if the rabbits were given away or if they died of natural causes or if they were lost in our backyard. Not knowing, according to Lucian, is terrible.

"Mom, your rabbits could be lost and they might be looking for you."

I love that Lucian is so sensitive and so compassionate with his pet. After all, isn't that what having a pet for our children is all about? I could've been one of those parents who get excited about buying a bunny in springtime when the toddlers go crazy over the idea of having a furry friend like the Easter Bunny. What can be more cute for a child? Yet beyond that first Easter, the rabbit will live up to eight years. Imagine that! That is longer than I was married to Lucian's dad. The truth is, we've had our Fluffy for four years, and there are times when I walk into the room and think I'm about to give up on her.

I've contemplated moving the cage somewhere else, but I've noticed that she really likes being around us. I feel terrible leaving her alone in a dark room, because rabbits are very social and they enjoying being petted often. One time I visited the home of a friend who had a bunny for the first time. The cute rabbit was tiny and his fur was black and white, and he seemed to enjoy the "suite" that his owners had placed him in. A large space, he had a whole room for himself; it even had wooden steps for him to climb. Wow, that bunny was set! I remember coming home that evening and looking at Fluffy's cage. I must buy a bigger home for you, Fluffy, I thought. Months passed, and Fluffy was still in her tiny cage. I saw my friend again at a dinner party and she told me that she had decided to give away the bunny. Too much poop.

However tempting it has been to get rid of our adorable pet, I will try to commit to it and show my son that even though I dread the duty sometimes (and I sure try to hide it the best I can), I will commit to our rabbit for the rest of her life. Then again, my mind is rolling with self-reproachful thoughts. I'm sure most parents don't overthink the issue of letting go of a pet all that much.

"Having a pet or a living thing aside from me and my son in this home has to account for something," I tell myself. Enter the idea of another living thing that nourishes my experience every day: plants.

I first learned about the love affair between women and plants from my mom. She always wanted to build a nursery in our backyard. Years later, when I moved to Atlanta, I would visit my friend Miranda's home and sense that she had a special power to keep plants alive and thriving. How did she do it? I'd wonder. She had a gift for taking care of plants. She'd move them from her porch into the living room when the season was about to change, and water them just the right way. I wish I could take care of my plants the way Miranda does. I have a few pots in my home, but I can't say that they are thriving.

I'm sitting in the living room at home, and like any other day I'm looking across the room to examine the state of my plants. They are making it okay. I'm far from an expert, but I love plants and the positive effect that having them in a home can bring. I especially like roses, any kind of roses, but the wild roses that I see around gardens throughout the year in Atlanta are just delightful to me.

The attention and respect that he feels for plants is something that Lucian has shown me since he was a toddler. Long gone are the days when he would pull petals off flowers. "Ouch," I'd say, and slowly he started appreciating what flowers meant, that they were for us as well as others to enjoy. As much as I have shown him how to treat plants, I'm so grateful to see that he has learned from school how to look at nature with eyes of appreciation. The principles of conservation and being conscious of protecting our planet are messages that children are open to at this early age. I haven't wasted a minute when

I've been given the chance to promote conservation, something that I deeply believe in.

I had been divorced for about two years when I decided that it was time to move out of the home I had shared with my son's dad and into a new place of my own. I was not so attached to the old home, but I *was* attached to the roses I had planted in front of the house. And so with my hand trowel, I dug out two rose bushes, talking to them the whole time. I explained that I wanted to bring them to my new home. To this day, I look at my rose bushes. Only one of the two has made it this far, and I feel that I did a good thing. I left behind so many memories in that house, but the roses remind me of the nurturing part of me that is still very much alive inside.

Although I'm unsure if I'm a plant person or not, I've continued to try to plant flowers in pots around our home. I water the plants hoping that they'll thrive. So far I've gotten mixed results since I moved to our current home, yet the bamboo palm and the philodendron have survived an astonishing two years. Plants can purify the air from toxins in the environment and can promote a more calming vibe in the home. I'm all over the idea of having a more calming environment, so I make sure that Lucian can come with me and choose a new plant every so often.

When I think about my plants I like to draw a parallel of circumstances: I notice how, in the same way that I water my plants and look after them, I should try to be attentive to my relationship with my son. I also think often about other relationships that make up what I call my "support system" in Atlanta. Beyond my family and the man that I love, I have to be attentive to my relationship with my dear friends, those who are close to my heart.

The end of the school year is a few weeks ahead. We'll soon be saying, "So long, second grade." Lucian and his friends are out of school and they are going to a play date at their friend Nathan's home. Nathan is Juliette's son, and I decide to come along and visit with Juliette while the kiddos play. Juliette's new home sits in a cul-de-sac, a modern house with dark brick and ivory siding. As you enter, the light-filled rooms greet you. On your left, along the windows of the dining room, there is a gallery of plants. Juliette takes me to the room as I ask the names of each plant: "What is this one called?"

Admittedly, I don't know much about plants, but these plants are unlike others. The energy in that room is palpable and as I walk around to learn the names, I feel the welcoming vibe. The leaves perfectly green, gleaming, the branches of the "money tree" in the corner almost reaching the window as if announcing that guests have arrived. Juliette moves around the room, stopping to describe each plant as if referring to a friend. The "butterfly" has various tones of bright colors throughout, its leaves with pointy corners and curves like butterfly wings. The hibiscus sits next to the dragon tongue across the room on top of a table, joined at the center of the dining room by a deep wine-colored calla lily, its flowers slowly opening up. All of them are vibrant, thriving, and, as Juliette explains, they each have a meaning.

"Do you talk to them, Juliette?"

"My mom does."

I could picture Juliette's mom talking with love and equanimity in this lovely home of her daughter's family. I had met her briefly once, and she was just as charming as her daughter. Juliette is a tall, gorgeous woman. Her black hair is shoulder length, thick and shining. Her skin is perfect, her eyes wide. She is smart and poised. A dentist, who was born in the Philippines and raised in Canada, she is practical and elegant, and her kind demeanor tells of someone who deeply cares. Her sweet disposition and generosity often come across before she has even said a word.

We decided to play chess with the children. Amanda, who had joined the boys at the play date, offered to play with me.

"Let's play here," I ventured. I wanted to take in all the good vibes that I could get from Juliette's delightful dining room.

A few days later at the local store, I was excited about getting new plants for our home, and I said to Lucian, "Let's plant these together." He looked puzzled, but he was agreeable to my idea. I wanted to promote the love of flowers and plants in my son. I hope that he sees in them a living thing, but I'm not sure that's something that comes naturally to children, so I feel that I must insist on fostering this connection with plants.

I enlisted Lucian's help as a gardener and he gladly agreed, for a small fee of a dollar or two. I've had this little boy watering my plants and helping around the house with chores that are less than appealing to any child. I've felt compelled to expand our moments of connection to times when we can learn from one another. When we are doing chores around the house, I get to talk to Lucian about things. Any conversation that will have him sharing his feelings is a great conversation for me. It takes a special moment and a certain mood for us to get into those conversations, but I love it when he shares his views on things and I patiently listen.

BECAUSE MOMS DON'T KNOW EVERYTHING

I had never heard of a hare. Or maybe I had, but I had no idea what exactly was the difference between a rabbit and a hare. So after consulting with Siri, we found ourselves looking at the infinite display of pictures of hares. Within a click or two, we had already found a detailed description of the species. While not exactly the same, hares are cousins of our rabbit, I explained as a follow-up to the more technical explanation that we found online. Hares live in places where the weather is colder, mom is learning as they both cuddle around the phone. My conversation with Lucian would go on and on. I was learning something new through my son's curiosity.

When did I feel like I know it all? I'm so grateful that we have technology that can help me along the way. I can't know everything and I don't expect to. But these days I find myself listening more to my son, understanding his point of view and where he is drawing his questions from. His questions often lead me to where his fears reside. Those questions are my guide, and even when sometimes I'm tired and I really don't feel like calling on Siri or looking for additional information to help find an answer to one of Lucian's newest areas of interest, I go there. I follow his cue. I realize if I let myself be led into his world, I will be surprised to find myself discovering something new every time.

Letting go of the control has been a dreadful "must do" in the past few years since my divorce. I've gone from knowing where I was to not knowing where I would be; my constant throughout these years has been my young son. My "North" has been the duty of being a mom, the desperate need to have that one thing in my life that I can feel extremely proud of having accomplished perfectly. It's only an illusion, I know.

There will be no rewards, no medals, no honors given to me. And who will be able to tell if I've been a good mom? It might be another subjective opinion up for discussion in the later years of my life. I'm trying my hardest to be the best mom that I can be to Lucian, and I should be okay with that. Yet my anxious mind will not rest until I'm finished, mentally speaking. It draws more energy from me because it gets me to a place where I'm thinking and thinking and planning ahead and revisiting my plans, of scrapping and scratching and drawing on the white board again for the tenth time. I can't take this plan of Lucian's life lightly. Nothing will ever be as important as making this master plan right.

And so if I'm to be his teacher, I'd better be a good one. I must know a bit of everything, at least. Literature, art, sports, music, even the despicable topic in my life: math. I've had to fake being good at it more than once, and I am not looking forward to the middle school years when teachers are going to start sending the hellish homework that I know I won't be able to understand. It's torture to think about what lies ahead in terms of homework. Science and math alike—I'd better line up the best tutors I can find for my son.

I wonder about the quality of my teachings, how much content and substance I'm providing my son. But regardless of the many teachings that I have for Lucian, he also is able to teach me some things. This is something that I firmly believe in. I'm reminded often through my son that there are lessons I must continuously face, and in learning those lessons I see that in the same way I show my son how to experience life, he too can show me a thing or two.

What exactly is he here to teach me? It doesn't take too long to discover areas where I could improve. I could be a better mom, I could be a better woman, I could be a better neighbor. It is in the wisdom of his words that sometimes I can clearly understand the lesson before my eyes.

My son teaches me about compassion when he asks me not to yell at the bunny when she is chewing off the floor molding. He teaches me about patience when it takes him a few more minutes to tie his shoes or buckle his belt. He teaches me about kindness when he wants to forgo soccer practice to spend time with his best friend because, like he says, "he never gets to play enough" with his buddy after school. He teaches me about manners when he opens the door for me, and he teaches me about forgiveness when, upon hearing any slight argument that I'm having with another adult, he asks that I "be nice." It is Lucian who teaches me about forgiving because it is through him that I am forced to strengthen my co-parenting skills.

"Life doesn't always go your way."

Lucian has taught me some of the most important lessons in my life so far. It's been a magical stage, these eight years. I can say that I now enjoy a more civilized son who can be wise at times, funny and smart, silly and rambunctious and highly energetic, cuddly and sensitive, all packed in to the handsome little boy that is Lucian. I look at the purple folder that we were handed on the first week of school back when Lucian started second grade.

The words SMART, KIND, FAST, FUNNY, TALL were

sorted playfully in different colors on the front of the folder. I couldn't believe it at first, but they nailed it. "That's Lucian, right there." I felt a sense of relief to know that my son's teachers really got who he was. Around this time Lucian started showing his preferences, developing skills and tastes and taking on ideas that might determine which turn he'll take in life when given the choice to make big decisions like going to college or starting a family. I want to be sure that I'm allowing the master in him to come out. I don't want to muzzle the greatness inside, and I have to be vigilant so that I don't crush his dreams, whatever they may be.

Since I know that I am an anxious mom whose actions can impact greatly my son's quality of life, I'm working hard at tamping myself down at the times when I'm stressed out. I'm going a bit slower and I'm listening more attentively. I'm seeing the results of my years of tackling my anxieties down. Taming the beast inside me has provided a peaceful and balanced experience for my son, and that is my greatest motivation to continue with my daily practice. Silence, mindfulness, patience, being present for my child, I am committed to listening more and more intently, to being more patient even when I feel that I don't have it in me, to be even more attentive, and to slow down.

Where I used to say to myself, "I think I know enough to be a great parent," I say instead, "I've found healing in silence." When I feel like I'm exhausted and don't have the energy to connect with my son, I push through and tell my anxious mind, "It is through connections that we heal." The journey has not been a smooth one, and it is clear to me that many unimaginable surprises are yet to be unveiled before me. I find comfort in knowing that I'm not alone, that I am enough, and that, as I tell Lucian so very often, "I am equipped, perfectly created by the power from above."

It has helped me discover areas of myself that I wasn't completely aware of in the past. As I attempt to get closer to my child, to connect with him in a meaningful way, I need to look closely at my own most hidden fears. I can always learn something new.

The strategies that I've put in place to heal my anxiety have brought new habits to my daily routine: embracing silence, slowing down, taking a break from the Web, releasing emotions that no longer serve me, staying physically fit, and being more mindful about my conversations are some of them. I've noticed that these strategies have helped me with other areas of my life. Beyond parenting, having more calm interactions with family, at work, and with friends has yielded new ways of communicating with and experiencing others. I've also discovered new activities and hobbies that I thoroughly enjoy and that energize my soul.

Learning to be a good parent is like signing up for a class that has no end date. There isn't a finish line or a textbook that will guide you through, and when you think you've adjusted to a season in parenting, a new stage reveals itself, requiring you to adjust again. There are always new areas to experience. Like a Super Mario Brothers video game, there is always a new level to enter where your abilities as a caregiver can evolve into a better version, every time.

I recently received the most wonderful note from Lucian's homeroom teacher. He had been named second grade's "Good

Samaritan" for his acts of kindness toward others at school. To say that I felt proud of my son is an understatement. Not only that, to expect that I should get all the credit for raising him in a way that has led him to be kind and generous and willing to help others would be pretentious on my part. It takes a tribe, and I have one: my friends and family and all the teachers who have shared their advice and insights, footprints that I've followed in spite of my anxious modes.

The unfriendly ghosts that create the anxiety that I want to rid myself of may be persistent. But the more I keep my anxiety under control, the more I'm able to teach my son the important "self" lessons that every child needs to learn: lessons of self-acceptance, self-love, self-discipline and self-exploration. Becoming a better mother takes discipline and a deep desire to be willing, and tenacious.

Healing from anxiety is possible. There are tools and resources that we can benefit from, and the results of incorporating habits that promote mindfulness in our lives are measurable. What is needed is the courage and the will to change old habits and replace them with new ones. It takes an open heart and an open mind to follow the path that can lead us to a more peaceful place in our hearts. When we find that peaceful place inside, we can become a more mindful woman, mother, aunt, friend, who lives a more abundant and joyful life.

Acknowledgments

I'm deeply grateful to my family, Adacelis Rivera Otero, Martín Iguina Mora, my brothers Emilio David Pérez and Emilio Luis Pérez and their families, my aunt and uncle Sonia Abruzzo and Douglas Abruzzo, and my extended family, Sebastián Otero, Anita Otero, Alfonso Otero, Alexandra Otero and Justin Roth; to my friends, Catalina and Brett Busch, Michele Barcelo, Kathleen Tantucco, and Chandler Cole; and to all of those who have in one way or another journeyed with me throughout the completion of this work. Also, I'll be forever grateful for the support of Johanna Hernández, Marilia Nieves, Carmen Ruiz, Eneris Medina, and Lucenith Cuevas. This book wouldn't be possible without the help of my editors, Marilyn Burkley and Erica Garvin, and the words of encouragement from Karen Kallis and Dorothy Sullivan.

I'm also grateful for the valuable feedback provided by Amesheia Buckner, Daniel DeNoon, Belsie González and Mark Helmy.

To all of you, thank you.

References

Introduction
    *Substance Abuse and Mental Health Services Administration statistics of incidence of generalized anxiety disorder (GAD) among women

    US Department of Health and Human Services,
    Office on Women's Health:
    https://www.womenshealth.gov/mental-health/mental-health-conditions/anxiety-disorders/

    National Institutes of Health Library of Publications:
    https://www.ncbi.nlm.nih.gov/pubmed/29866128

    **Anxiety in women, a Swedish national three-generational cohort study. Authors: Sydsjö G1, Agnafors S2, Bladh M3, Josefsson A3. (Sweeden, 2018)

Chapter 2. Healing My Heart
    Spiritual Divorce, Debbie Ford
    Living with Anxiety, Carolyn Chambers Clark

Chapter 3. Connecting with My Son
    The Gifts of Imperfection, Dr. Brené Brown
    The Power of Now, Eckhart Tolle
    The Awakened Family, Dr. Shefali Tsabary

Chapter 5. Breathe Away the Pain

How to Behave So Your Children Will, Too! Sal Severe

Have You Filled a Bucket Today? Carol McCloud

The 5 Love Languages of Children, Gary Chapman and Ross Campbell

Mind Whispering, Tara Bennett-Goleman

Chapter 6. Build a Bridge

The Life-Changing Magic of Tidying, Marie Kondo

The Cyber Effect, Mary Aiken

The Four Agreements, Don Miguel Ruiz

Successful Sleep Strategies for Kids, Dennis Rosen

The Marshmallow Test, Walter Mischel

Chapter 7. Teaching through Example

Anxious, Joseph LeDoux

Raising Resilient Children, Robert Brooks and Sam Goldstein

The Tapping Solution, Alex Ortner

Chapter 8. Ahead of the Wave

The Cyber Effect, Mary Aiken

The Wishing Year, Noelle Oxenhandler

The Power of Now, Eckhart Tolle

How to Behave so Your Children Will, Too! Sal Severe

About the Author

Adacelis Pérez is an author, certified life coach, and communications professional with a passion for mindful parenting. She has worked as a publicist for internationally renowned news anchors, orchestrated major public relations and social marketing campaigns, and helped develop successful communications programs for leading brands across the world. She is a two-time recipient of a certificate of contribution from Peabody Awards for her collaboration in CNN's coverage of the Arab Spring and Hurricane Katrina. Both bilingual and bicultural, she was born in Puerto Rico, and has called Atlanta, Georgia, home for the past twenty years, where she lives with her young son, Lucian, and their rabbit, Fluffy.

Website: AdacelisPerez.com
Twitter: @adacelisperez

Index

A

Aiken, Mary, 119-120, 193

Antidepressants, 49–51

Arecibo, 20, 23, 31, 41, 156, 158, 164

B

Belonging, 118-119

Bennett-Goleman, Tara, 160

Breathing exercises, 87, 128-129, 137-138

Brooks, Robert, 163

Brown, Brené, 67

C

Candida (candidiasis), 20, 78–80

Chopra, Deepak, 60

Clark, Carolyn Chambers, 59

CNN, 35-36, 73-75

Community, 119, 156-157, 204-205

Compassion, 8, 42, 68, 100, 110, 223

Connection, 7-10, 60, 67, 108, 141, 224

D

Decluttering, 116-118, 130

Depression, 51, 172

Divorce, 39–40, 44–47, 50, 59

Dyer, Wayne, 145, 152, 233

E

Eczema, 69-70

EFT (tapping), 168-172

Emotion, 5–7, 10, 58–59, 65, 80-81, 100, 104, 131–134, 139-140, 152, 166, 168

Encouragement, 134, 150, 160, 172

Exercise, 46, 52, 171, 179-180

Exercises, breathing 87, 108, 128-129, 137-138

F

Fajardo, Puerto Rico, 24
Family dynamics, 100
Family, anxiety's effects on, 7, 90
Feeling safe, 100
Ford, Debbie, 39

G

Generalized anxiety, 6, 10, 98, 104
Genetic factors, 55, 100
Goldstein, Sam, 163
Gratitude, 124,138

H

Hay, Louise, 172
Humility, 156-157
Hurricanes, 1, 202

J

Journalists, 34-35
Judgment, 67

K

Kallis, Karen, 103

Kondo, Marie, 116

M

Medication, 10, 17–20, 109-110, 166
Meditation, 4, 77, 88, 104, 129, 138
Mindfulness, 8, 60, 172, 179

O

Oxenhandler, Noelle, 196

P

Parenting, 16, 48, 147-148, 155, 189, 192
Pets, 93, 182, 213
Pope Francis, 81
Puerto Rico, 1, 3, 8, 164, 202

R

Rosen, Dennis, 113

S

Severe, Sal, 147, 197
Social media, 9, 106, 118, 176, 209
Stress, 6, 37, 103, 109, 114, 128, 138, 151, 166, 172
Support, 114, 174, 191, 218

T

Technology, 10, 118-119, 221

Tolle, Eckhart, 152

U

University of Puerto Rico, 164

V

Vacation, 24–26, 163

Volunteering, 20, 33, 156

Y

Yoga, 37, 104, 113, 131

CPSIA information can be obtained
at www.ICGtesting.com
Printed in the USA
LVHW111649250421
685526LV00006B/994